LITTLE READERS,
Big Thinkers

Teaching
Close Reading
in the **Primary Grades**

LITTLE READERS,
Big Thinkers

Teaching
Close Reading
in the Primary Grades

AMY STEWART

FOREWORD BY STEVEN L. LAYNE

 Stenhouse
PUBLISHERS

PORTLAND, MAINE

Stenhouse Publishers
www.stenhouse.com

Credits
Cover: Alessandra S. Turati; photograph ©Dynamicfoto-PedroCampos/iStock Images
Figures 3.13, 4.5, and 4.6: "Illustrations," by Christian Robinson, copyright © 2014 by Christian Robinson; and Excerpt(s) from *The Smallest Girl in the Smallest Grade* by Justin Roberts, copyright © 2014 by Justin Roberts. Used by permission of G. P. Putnam's Sons Books for Young Readers, an imprint of Penguin Young Readers Group, a division of Penguin Random House LLC. All rights reserved.
Figures 3.3, 3.5, and 4.1: From *Recess at 20 Below* by Cindy Lou Aillaud, © copyright 2005, reprinted by Permission from Alaska Northwest Books.
Tables on pages 73, 89, and 97 adapted from *Text-Dependent Questions* (Fisher and Frey 2014b).
Appendix F: "I Am a Pizza," written by Peter Alsop, © copyright 1983, Moose School Music (BMI). On *Wha'DYa Wanna Do?* For more songs by Peter check out www.peteralsop.com.

Cover design, interior design, and typesetting: Alessandra S. Turati

Library of Congress Cataloging-in-Publication Data
Names: Stewart, Amy, 1987- author.
Title: Little readers, big thinkers : teaching close reading in the primary
    grades / Amy Stewart.
Description: Portsmouth, NH : Stenhouse Publishers, 2018. | Includes
    bibliographical references.
Identifiers: LCCN 2018055320 (print) | LCCN 2018027709 (ebook) | ISBN
    9781625312129 (pbk. : alk. paper) | ISBN 9781625312136 (ebook)
Subjects: LCSH: Reading (Primary) | Reading comprehension—Study and teaching
    (Primary)
Classification: LCC LB1525 .S78 2018 (ebook) | LCC LB1525 (print) | DDC
    372.4—dc23
LC record available at https://lccn.loc.gov/2018055320

Manufactured in the United States of America

PRINTED ON 30% PCW
RECYCLED PAPER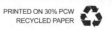

25 24 23 22 21 20 19   9 8 7 6 5 4 3 2 1

To Mom and Dad, for being my first teachers.

To Terry, for your unwavering belief in me.

contents

foreword

I first knew the author of the book you are holding in your hand or perusing on your electronic device as Amy Kempf. She was my student— not my kindergarten student, not one of my fifth graders or eighth graders

. . . a great big no to all of that. She was my master's student, and she was a standout, as I imagined, even back then, she had probably been in every educational situation in which she ever participated. Amy's writing voice was solid—our entire faculty spotted it immediately. No surprise that, with a little of what we in the Literacy Department at Judson University call nudging (and the students refer to as frightening intimidation), she published her first article in a peer-reviewed journal: "Conferring with Kindergarten Writers: They're More than Just Illustrators" (2013. *Illinois Reading Council Journal* 41(3): 22–29).

And then there was the essay that I suggested she write for assignment credit in a course I was teaching: "Making Time for Reflection: One Teacher's Quest Toward Deeper Student Understanding" (2014. *The Reading Teacher* 67(7): 527).

Amy's ability to command the stage as a speaker was also evidenced that year—and a little more encouragement from some of us might have led her to draft and submit a proposal to speak at the Illinois Reading Council Conference the following year where she literally WOWED the CROWD! She's speaking there nearly every year now.

Long story short—now she's Amy Stewart and has a wonderfully supportive husband and family, an ever-growing fan base (the more she presents . . . the more they love her), a doctoral cohort and faculty at Judson University who count themselves among her biggest cheerleaders and who are already prepping their "I knew her when . . ." elevator speeches, and me. She has me. 100 percent. I'm all in. I'll go to the mat for her anytime, anywhere. I'll use any influence I have to help her, and you're not surprised, right? Because it's what teachers do. Moreover, look in the mirror and try to tell yourself it's not exactly what you would do if she were your student. It's why you . . . and I . . . and Amy Stewart became teachers! We want to see our students soar—and when we chose this profession, we committed to doing all that we could to help them get there. So, I need you to know that Amy didn't ask me to write the foreword to her book and neither did Bill "Obi-Wan Kenobi" Varner, our editor. No, I offered. Just like you would have. Because (say it with me) . . . "that's what teachers do."

And I'm so glad I did. It has been quite a few years since I was working full-time, day-in, day-out, in a primary classroom; however, Amy's book put me right back there. Her conversational style is so appealing—you will LOVE it—and you will feel you've made a new friend. It will be clear from the opening pages that she "gets it," and that's what we are always looking for in a strong professional book. For primary teachers who may have had some trepidation about how to employ close reading success-fully: your worries are over! In this book, Amy lays out not only the rationale, the "why," but moreover she clearly and simply articulates the "how" to facilitate close reading with little learners in very tangible and reader-friendly ways.

I found myself laughing aloud at times while I was reading, and I marked up the manuscript in several places because so many of her suggestions and illustrations were brilliant! I knew that you, her readers, would be scrambling to use them and to share them with your colleagues! Again and again in this book, Amy calls on you to make the decisions that are best for your little readers, but she also empowers you to better understand that much of what you are already doing can be gently morphed into close reading experiences that can capitalize on your readers' interests and expand their skills. Her sample lessons, aligned to the CCSS (in case that really lights you up) provide tremendous exemplars of how to manage repeated readings as well as how to assist young learners in citing textual evidence, expanding their vocabulary, and employing both writing and drawing as they respond to the close reading of a text.

It is my great pleasure to invite you inside the teaching life of a young woman I truly believe was born to do what she is doing: help kids and help teachers. Congratulations—you are about to be able to say, "I was with her from her very first book!" And eventually "Oh, yes, I followed Amy from way back—I have all of her books!" Maybe even someday, "I had a coffee with her at ILA, and she is just so real. I'm a fan for life!" But let's just remember one thing about her fan base, everybody—and it's important—I was first. Teach the children . . . and treat them well.

— Steven L. Layne

acknowledgments

Writing often seems like a lonely endeavor, but when you take a closer look, you reflect on and remember everyone who makes that writing possible. There are so many people whose incredible generosity and knowledge have shaped my thinking and the content of this—my very first—book (still can't believe this is real life). So much of writing a book, in my opinion, is surrounding yourself with good snacks and with the best, most encouraging people. These are my people.

I owe so much gratitude to the team at Stenhouse, without whom this book would not exist. Thank you to Bill Varner, for holding this first-time author's hand every step of the way. Your belief in my work, your guidance, and your expert wordsmithing have been invaluable to me—I'm glad to know you. To Chandra Lowe—thank you for answering every one of my questions with an entertaining and perfectly punctuated style that only an English major could pull off, and for providing me with a sense of belonging and friendship as I learned the ropes of authorship. Thanks also to Grace Makley, Louisa Irele, and everyone on the production team who worked to make this book—with all its tables, photos, and permissions—a reality.

The experiences and opportunities I have had as a teacher have been made possible by several wonderful people. I have worked with, learned from, and been inspired by some truly amazing educators. To Missy Fairs, for showing me with utmost selflessness how to be a teacher so many years ago, and to Marianne Hackler and Krista Verba, who uplifted and supported me when I first became one, thank you.

I am forever indebted to my BSD2 colleagues, especially Armando Campos, Kay Dugan, Liz Fausto, Christina Guevara, Kelly Kendall, Sarah

Milic, Terri Schwabe, Brooke Smith, Rachael Tortorello, and Ben Zulauf, who believe in my work and who have been instrumental in helping me refine and polish my ideas and my writing. I am grateful to work and learn alongside such dedicated and collaborative educators. Thank you also to Melissa Wallace, Lynda Gatto, Vicky Eltman, and Nancy Bomicino, who pulled countless library books for me and were so kind when I turned them in late. And, to Amber Reedy, my favorite colleague from afar.

To DLIT4, my doctoral cohort at Judson University: Stasia (who must be listed first), Cindi, Elizabeth, Mal, Kirby, Stacie, and Stephanie—your love and partnership mean the world to me. I love you all right back. Your collective passion for reading, writing, and leading will change the world.

To Dr. Steven Layne, for being the first person to ever tell me I was a good writer—thank you. Your belief in me has made me believe in myself. Thank you for writing the foreword to this book, and for all the other big and small ways you have shown you are in my corner.

Finally, writing (and finishing!) this book would not have been possible without my family. Thank you to the Stewarts, for welcoming me into your family with open arms, for always asking about my writing, and for not judging when I eat more than my fair share of cheese and crackers at Sunday dinner.

To Mom, Dad, Christopher, Corey, Nicholas, and Eric—you will always be my favorite people. Thank you for loving me and for being a constant source of laughter and motivation. I promise I will learn how to play euchre some day.

And, of course, to Terry. I am lucky to be living life with you.

1

Little Readers, Big Thinking: A Case for Close Reading in K–2

We won't stop digging until we find something spectacular.
—MAC BARNETT, *SAM AND DAVE DIG A HOLE*

■ Introduction

It's a typical day in kindergarten. Students are hard at work reading and writing during workshop time. I walk over to check in on David, who, I notice, is sprawled on his back on the corner rug, a book about monster trucks covering his face, pencil and sticky notes close by, but not within reach and definitely not in use. Something tells me that he's either asleep under there or just killing time until lunch. I'll just go give him a quick redirection. I ask him how it's going with his reading today, expecting either no response or something quick and dismissive, like "it's good." Instead I get, "Shhhh Mrs. Stewart . . . I'm thinking. Don't you know I do good thinking when I'm like this?" Silly me, I guess! So I sit down, lean in close, and listen to David as, sure enough, he tells me all about his monster truck thinking and what he had been noticing and learning about them in his book. I learn an important lesson that day—that kids are always thinking and that thinking is always happening, even when your teacher eyes don't really know for sure, and even when you least expect it.

Walk into any primary-grade classroom and you'll likely witness a lot of thinking—students thinking as they add new learning to a chart in the science center, students thinking as they mark their choice for hot lunch (sometimes it's a tough one!), students thinking as they choose new books from the classroom library, students thinking as they debate whether the teacher will let them go to the bathroom . . . again. Whether it's the beginning of the year in kindergarten, or the end of the year in second grade, thinking is happening nonstop. And it is exactly this nonstop thinking that calls us to provide reading opportunities that let students unleash their thinking, showing all they know and all they are capable of knowing.

Close reading is a tool that helps us harness the big thinking we know is inside the little minds that fill our classrooms with brilliance each day. The concept and process of close reading challenges us to teach our students new ways to enjoy texts as we work alongside them and nudge them toward a deeper level of comprehension. As primary-grade teachers, we are capable of empowering our students—from their earliest years of school—to think about and engage with texts in ways that will set them up for success as the readers, writers, and thinkers of the future. We must start our students on the path toward becoming close and careful readers now, even when they're little, because sometimes even our littlest readers are also our biggest thinkers.

■ An Affirmation

This book begins with an affirmation of what you are already doing. I know the work of a primary-grade teacher. I know you are getting to school early, staying late, working through your lunch (and specials and recess), and doing everything that is humanly possible to make a difference for your students. I get it. I live it. When you are already doing so much by way of planning learning opportunities, it is easy to think of close reading as something new and completely separate from the reading opportunities you currently make possible in your classroom—as just another thing to add to your never-ending to-do list. But I want you to realize as we move forward together that many of those reading opportunities into which you pour your passion actually already are close reading. I'm hopeful that there are at least a few instances where you will think, I already do that! Close reading takes those instructional moves to the next level, deepening the learning outcomes and challenging your readers to notice and say more about a text.

Just as some of your classroom practices already fit with close reading, so too do many of the books you love to read. Primary-grade teachers love our books, and the good news is that close reading doesn't mean you have to give up the books you love—I promise! Many of your favorites will lend themselves well to being closely read alongside your students. Implementing close reading strategies will help you to notice and discover even more to love within the pages of your most cherished books.

In this book, we think about the reading opportunities we provide for our students and then look at those experiences in a new light as we decide where they fit or how we can deepen them by using close reading strategies. Get excited, people. We're making close reading fun again.

■ What Close Reading Is . . . and What It Isn't

When we primary-grade teachers think about close reading, many of our minds immediately fill with visions of middle-grade students hunched over difficult passages, scrawling lengthy annotations in the margins, writing elaborate responses to text-dependent questions, or doing other scary things that our little readers and writers are simply not ready to tackle (nor should they be). These preconceived notions about what close reading must look like cause much of our resistance or hesitance to teach our students about it. We know that our young students may not yet even be able to write, let alone provide written responses and annotations, so if these things are such a big part of close reading, how can we manage them in the first years of school (Figure 1.1)?

What I've learned from my favorite close reading experts, including Kylene Beers, Robert Probst, Doug Fisher, Nancy Frey, Chris Lehman, and Kate Roberts, is that close reading can take on many forms, and that how we use close reading very much depends on the readers with whom we learn each day. When we think about close reading with young children, we are really thinking about teaching them how to engage and interact with a text by demonstrating the practices of close reading and inviting students to practice using close reading strategies in a way that will move them forward as readers. I certainly agree that we need to keep students' developmental readiness and present levels of performance at the forefront of instruction; however, we must be careful with the mind-set that because students are young, they are unable to think deeply about the words and ideas presented in a text. We cannot use "developmentally appropriate" as a default excuse that excludes younger students from developing close reading strategies

Figure 1.1
Kindergartners listen to *Sam and Dave Dig a Hole* before learning about close reading.

that allow them to engage in deep thinking, collaborative conversations, and new understandings surrounding a text. Similarly, close reading allows young readers to transact (Rosenblatt 1978) with a challenging text that may not otherwise be accessible to them.

If we exclude close reading from our literacy instruction, we may be unknowingly or inadvertently sending the message to students that reading is not much more than word calling through the pages just to get to the end, to pick up another book, and to do it all over again. Conversely, including close reading practices as part of reading instruction at certain points throughout the year calls attention to a new, different kind of reading—one where students begin to understand that they can read a text multiple times in order to learn more about an author's craft and purpose, to engage in metacognitive practices, and to form new understandings.

■ A Place for Close Reading in K–2

The literacy learning opportunities we provide for our primary-grade students are unique, differing from those in the middle and upper grades. It is understandable to wonder, since our repertoire of essential instructional practices in literacy is already bursting at the seams. Why we should even be thinking about adding on something else. Do we really need close reading? It's a valid question, and one that often plagues early-elementary teachers (myself included) as they contemplate the value of close reading in a classroom filled with early and emergent readers. But the close reading that we experience with our young readers supports several aspects of their literacy development, especially comprehension, and makes it an essential component of literacy instruction, even in the first years of school.

■ Reading to Learn

Jeanne Chall (1983) points out that often primary-grade teachers put an emphasis on learning to read over reading to learn, which is understandable given the nature of our everyday work. We do so much important work teaching students how to read that it is easy to forget about teaching them what to do with their reading ability, especially when we have to remember who rides which bus, whose turn it is to be student of the week, and who has been to the bathroom four times already today. The truth is, if the only books that are put in front of children are those at their "reading level," we may be stifling their thinking. When we teach students about new topics, new words, and new ideas using close reading, they are exposed to new types of texts that expand their thinking about what reading is and about what readers do. Nancy Frey (Fisher and Frey 2014a) cautions that the kinds of texts students can read independently in the early years of school do not have the complexity to support deep thinking. It is our job to make accessible to our little readers texts that do support deep thinking.

Taking the advice of Lindsey Moses (Moses and Ogden 2017), we can create an environment where learning to read and reading to learn happen alongside one another, and we can use close reading as a means to make it happen. For example, a first grader might spend much of her day working to solidify decoding and word work skills during independent, guided, and shared reading opportunities, which would be classified as learning to read. Supplementing that with reading to learn, that same first grader would also have supported interactions with texts that are above her reading level in order to expand her thinking around first-grade texts and topics. Teaching young readers to be examiners of text allows them to apply what they know about how to read to why they are reading.

■ The Power of Talk

Making talk part of the close reading experience opens up amazing learning and thinking experiences for our young students. The most crucial result of close reading is a deep, individual understanding of a text using transferable skills and strategies. While students in middle and upper grades are more equipped to demonstrate this understanding through writing, it would be inauthentic to ask our young students to write extensive, elaborate annotations or responses to reading if they are not yet ready to do so. Our students can, however, express the depth of their understanding by talking about their thinking during collaborative conversations and discussions with peers (see Figure 1.2). Text-focused comprehension conversations allow young students to share their thinking and new learning about a text and connect it to the thinking of their peers. Through these conversations they are able to build or solidify a true understanding of a text. Maria Walther's words ring true: "Collaborative conversations are the glue that cements the learning" (2015, 102).

The idea that student talk is essential for comprehension is not a new one. James Britton (1970, 164) writes that our classrooms should "float on a sea of talk." This "sea" is especially imperative during close reading experiences. Allowing students time to engage in text-centered talk strengthens their initial understanding of a text because it requires them to interpret their own meaning, share this meaning with their peers, and participate in a dialogue about a particular piece of text.

The following conversation took place in a second-grade classroom after reading the book *One Plastic Bag: Isatou Ceesay and the Recycling Women of the Gambia* by Miranda Paul (2015). A group of students was discussing a student-generated question based on this narrative-nonfiction text.

> **Student 1:** *This book made me think about plastic bags in America. Why do you think that some places let you use plastic bags but other places do not?*
>
> **Student 2:** *I think maybe because they don't know about the trash in the oceans.*
>
> **Student 3:** *Maybe if they knew about it we wouldn't have plastic bags. We would just have the kind that you use over again.*
>
> **S1:** *But if we know about it and we are kids, then adults should know about it.*
>
> **Student 4:** *Maybe this book is trying to tell us that we can spread the word.*

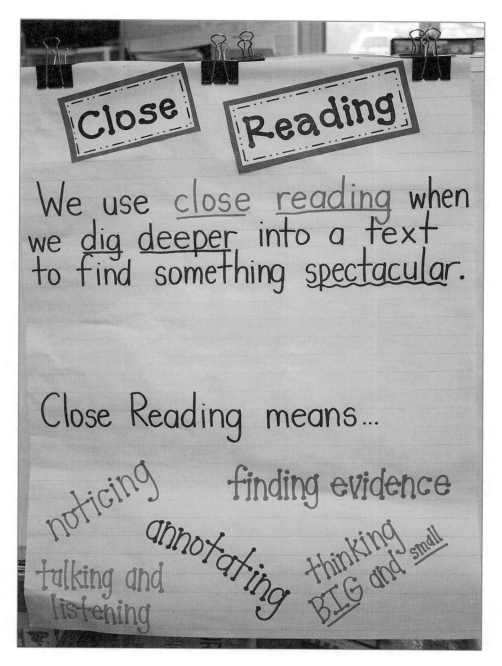

Figure 1.2
Use a chart to define close reading for young readers.

S3: I agree. If more places know about the plastic, I bet they wouldn't use as much.

S1: It is really hurting the world.

This particular conversation went on to inspire some social action within the school community surrounding the use of plastic.

While it is important to point out that student talk such as this does not happen overnight, this conversation exemplifies the level of comprehension that can take place through the use of spoken close reading with K–2 students.

◼ Letting Students Have the Stage

Before a read-aloud, teachers naturally preview the text with students, frontloading any tricky words, introducing new concepts, and providing any information needed to understand the text. Sometimes, by the time I am done previewing a book, ten minutes have passed and I'm the only one who has done any talking or thinking. Just ask Aiden, sitting at the back of the class and ever-so-slyly twisting Julia's hair into knots. With close reading there is limited frontloading (Fisher and Frey 2012), which requires the students to do more of the thinking. If we step out of the spotlight and let our students have the stage, they are able to think for themselves, rather than think about what *we* want them to think about. This is just one more way to let our young readers do the challenging reading-is-thinking work, instead of our doing it for them. The earlier we can invite students to develop their own thinking, the sooner they are able to gain and share new knowledge.

◼ Close Reading and Inquiry Learning

Inquiry instruction, according to Harvey Daniels, is "building instruction out of children's curiosity" (2017, xi). If your students are anything like mine, their curiosity is seemingly limitless. Our little learners are full of questions and wonderings, so much so that sometimes they need a focal point or topic to guide their curiosity. That focal point can come from the student thinking that follows careful close reading work with young learners.

At the heart of inquiry learning are observation and wonder. Close reading can provide the platform for such observation and wonder to take place, because student wonderings that arise from a close reading experience invite further noticing, research, looking closely, and lingering (Mraz, Porcelli, and Tyler 2016). Because they are learning to be close and critical readers, students—yes, even (and especially) primary-grade students—can take ownership of their learning and find the answers they are seeking through inquiry experiences.

Take the example of the book *One Plastic Bag* (Paul 2015) mentioned earlier in the second-grade comprehension conversation. Learning from this text through multiple readings allowed students to form opinions, take stances, and, most importantly, ask questions. Because we took the time as a class to give this text the attention it deserved, my students were able to craft their own learning experiences based on what they still wanted to know or what this book inspired them to do. One group of students wanted to do more research about plastic pollution, while another group of students wanted to stand on Isatou's shoulders as they learned more about what they could create by repurposing plastic bags. These are just two examples of student-driven learning that came about because of close reading, but the possibilities are endless!

Close reading and inquiry experiences go hand in hand as students use their learning from a text to help them solve a problem, answer a question, or simply find out more. Certainly student inquiry can take place without close reading, but the deep reading of a text often gives student inquiry a launching point, which can be especially helpful in the primary grades.

■ K–2 Close Reading as a Stepping Stone

Finally, you can think of K–2 close reading as a stepping-stone to the reading that will take place as students get older. It is our job as primary teachers to expose students to close reading so that when they get to the middle and upper grades, they are able to own these practices and use them more independently. Just as we prepare them to read just-right books or to master grade-level math concepts before sending them off to the next grade, so too must we prepare our little learners to be critical, thoughtful readers.

Using Pearson and Gallagher's (1983) model of the gradual release of responsibility, close reading in the early years of school often means saying, "I do" and "We do." As students get older, the "I do" and "We do" become "You do." If we do nothing by way of fostering close reading skills, we fail to set our students up for success and independence with the kinds of reading and thinking they will do in the future.

There are a few things that we as primary-grade teachers can keep in mind as we begin to think about using close reading experiences with our students. The first is that close reading is a not a lesson plan—a one-and-done experience or something to be planned once and repeated over time—

but a strategy that we call on throughout the year to deepen students' under-standing. It is a variety of fluid practices that guide readers to interact with and think about any text or topic in a new and deeper way. Close reading allows young learners to think critically about a text, demonstrate that thinking in a way that is meaningful for them, and share that thinking with peers and adults. It adds another layer to literacy instruction and provides an arena in which students can apply the reading and writing skills they have learned while adding new skills to their toolboxes.

With that being said, it is not a strategy or practice that you will engage in with your young readers every single day, or every single week (cue sighs of relief). Rather, it should be used purposefully and strategically as needed with students to move their thinking forward about a text or idea. We don't have to use it all the time! We can still read books just for fun! By expecting too many close reading experiences, we lose volume in terms of the students' exposure to text, and our students lose the stamina of vora-cious readers.

Another thing to keep in mind is that close reading is just one piece of your balanced literacy instruction. Doug Fisher and Nancy Frey (2012, 180) remind us, "Close reading must be accompanied by other essential instruc-tional practices that are vital to reading development." You can bet that any primary-grade teacher's day is crammed full of reading and writing opportu-nities. From read-aloud in the morning, to letter-sound practice in the lunch line, to a sight-word song on the way out the door in the afternoon, literacy is our jam. We know how important phonemic awareness and phonics skills are for our little readers. We know that knowledge of high-frequency words propels them forward, and that concepts of print, letter formation, and word building are all essential components of literacy instruction in the first years of school. Close reading does not—and should not—replace these things. What close reading should do is provide a context in which these skills can be practiced, applied, and transferred into real reading experiences. We are not forgetting about phonemic awareness, phonics, or word study, but rather folding those things into a close reading experience.

For example, students can annotate a text with a phonics or word study focus in mind. Instead of annotating for meaning or clarity, young readers can mark up a text by locating specific letters, words, or word chunks (see Figure 1.3). Differentiating between or identifying types of sentences can also be a focus of annotation for students working to secure that particular skill. Likewise, close reading can also be used to find mentor sentences or passages for use during writing workshop. As you or your students notice an author's move that could be replicated in students' writing, call attention to it and use it as an instructional piece during a writing minilesson. While using close reading strategies with an informational article, my students and I noticed that the text was separated into sections, each with a different heading. This is a structure that my students could choose to use when writing their own informational pieces. We were able to revisit this same article during writing workshop and examine the text structure even further.

Figure 1.3
A kindergarten student annotates the text by searching for specific letters and words.

Finally, our little readers need our guidance and support throughout most—if not all—of the close reading process. Close reading is not simply putting a too-hard text in front of students and then subsequently pulling our hair out when they don't "get it." Rather, as Fisher, Frey, and Lapp say, "The habit of close reading . . . doesn't simply develop—it must be purposefully taught, beginning in the first years of school" (2011, 5). Fisher and Frey (2014a) give permission for teachers to be the reader of the text in the primary grades, going so far as to call close reading in the early grades close listening. We support students as they think about and talk about texts that we have made accessible to them through reading aloud, and we provide scaffolds for success all along the way. We teach them what close reading means and show them what close readers do. Our students are always working toward independence with close reading, but we must know and understand that this independence may not be reached during the primary years of school. That's okay. While the readers in front of us may not yet be able to read the text we have chosen, they can transfer the skills and strategies we are using to uncover big ideas and new understandings. Exposing students to close reading and supporting them as they try out deeper reading strategies will set them up for future reading success and expand their capabilities as readers.

■ Close Reading and the Common Core State Standards

They say you never forget where you were or what you were doing when big events take place. That's sort of how it was with the Common Core State Standards for me. The year was 2010. I had felt I was finally getting a handle on this teaching thing. As we teachers were going about our merry ways, our new (albeit forced) BFFs, the standards, burst into our lives. True, we knew they were coming, but that somehow did not make the transition (read: panic) any easier. Read closely, they said. It will be fun, they said. The CCSS shifted a lot of what I thought I knew. Close reading, complex texts, and evidence-based thinking became everyday topics in our schools, leaving many of us wondering how to make sense of them all in relation to our young readers.

Somewhere along the way—perhaps in our frenzy to learn the standards, unpack the standards, teach the standards, and meet the standards—close reading got turned and twisted into something too hard and too scary to use with young readers. We lost ourselves in these new expectations before we even gave ourselves a chance to think about their implications in our classrooms. Now that we've been working with the CCSS or other higher-level standards for several years, we understand their rigor and complexity a little more and are better able to understand how to make these higher standards attainable for our students.

The truth is, while the standards have mandated many of the end-of-year outcomes of our teaching, they have not regulated how we go about reaching those outcomes with our students. This is both good and less good, in my opinion. On one hand, the Common Core puts its trust in teachers to design instruction and learning opportunities that enable students to read and analyze complex texts, understand those texts both explicitly and inferentially, and provide text evidence that supports their thinking. We are trusted (at least by the Common Core) to—get this—teach! On the other hand, we are often left wondering if we're doing it right, or if our students are meeting the standards as intended.

Keep in mind, though, that while standards may come and go, best practices endure. The instructional moves we know to be best for our students are not tied to standards, and we should not waver from good practice just to meet a standard. We know that what is best for our youngest readers is an environment where these complex and mind-stretching reading opportunities are nestled within scaffolds of support such as shared reading experiences and guided, collaborative conversations.

■ The Close Reading Process

What I love about the process of close reading is that there is no "right" way to go about it. It will look different depending on your students and the texts you choose to use with them. Think of close reading as a process that follows the needs and interests of your readers, and the opportunities to engage in the process will unfold naturally through carefully chosen texts.

We're so used to checking boxes and crossing things off to meet a standard expectation that we inadvertently anticipate that our close reading instruction must fit into a specific mold or formula. Continuous and formulaic repeated readings of texts have the potential to create a mundane experience that can chip away at students' love of reading. I've seen close reading experiences become so mechanized and repetitive that the students are bored, the teacher is frustrated, and the learning is forced (if it happens at all). This has happened to me, and I don't want it to happen to you. I am a fan of Nancy Boyles's thinking that close reading should "motivate as well as educate" (2014, 32).

Implementing close reading should not feel forced or cause us to lose the authenticity and ingenuity of our instruction. You've likely learned not to make the readers in your classroom do anything that you wouldn't organically do as an adult reader. Do I, as an adult, fill out a reading log? No. Do I take a test? No. Do I want to talk about it with my friends? Yes! Do I want to keep notes about it? Yes! Do I want to read it again? Yes! Close reading experiences are real reading experiences. Close reading is what real readers do. When provided with authentic opportunities for close reading that transfer to their real reading lives, students want to keep reading, learning, and thinking as their understanding takes shape.

That being said, there are a few pillars of the process to keep in mind whenever you think about close reading.

■ Multiple Readings

The first pillar of close reading is multiple or repeated readings of a text. In order to uncover layers of understanding, students must have multiple experiences with a book, article, or other piece of text. Many literacy experts agree that rereading a text is one of the best ways for students to improve comprehension.

I think the word *repeat* gets a bad rap, especially because no one likes whining, and hearing "We're doing this AGAIN?" from students is enough to make your skin crawl. When I was first learning about close reading, repeated readings were one of things that I was not crazy about trying. Primary-grade students are always on the move (both physically and mentally), so sticking to any one thing for too long has the makings of a classroom meltdown written all over it. I mean, it's a good day if we can get through the rest of reading workshop after someone has discovered an ant on the floor. Short attention spans and wiggly bodies made me dread returning to a text for a second, third, or (gasp!) even fourth time, but I quickly saw in my students' thinking the benefit of using the same text across multiple reading experiences.

As I started to accept the idea of repeated readings, I turned to myself as a reader—when would I reread something? This led me down a path of rereading for enjoyment, rereading for understanding, or rereading to inspire further learning or even further reading. If I return to a text as an adult reader and find it helpful, perhaps there is some value in returning to a text or piece of a text with my students. Okay, fine, I'll do it. The trick is to make returning to a text so exciting, engaging, and purposeful that students don't even think about raising their hands to tell you they've already heard this one. Consider what you love about rereading a text or a part of a text, and bring that joy to your students. If you haven't noticed, they pretty much love to do anything you love to do.

I've come to find that each reading of a text uncovers a deeper layer of comprehension and contributes to the "big thinking" outcome of a close reading experience. Debbie Miller's *Reading with Meaning* (2012) makes the case for repeated reading when she points out to students that their schema and understanding have grown because they returned to a text for different purposes. If my students had heard *One Plastic Bag* just one time, it would have been a nice read-aloud that led to a surface-level discussion, but because we revisited pieces of the text over multiple days, my students were able to grab ahold of concepts and ideas that moved them forward as learners and allowed them to think about making a difference in their own small way. When we invite and encourage multiple readings of a text, we help our students make meaning more profoundly and in different ways.

There is no set amount of readings that is standard across the board or that works with every reader in every classroom. A text that lends itself to three readings with one group of students may require five readings with another group. And different texts require varying degrees of "digging deeper," so the amount time spent with them will differ. Try not to feel as though your close reading experiences must be limited solely to a first, second, and third reading. It is easy to fall into a formulaic pattern, meaning a set number of readings and the same corresponding learning opportunities; the only thing that changes is the text. While this is a good starting point (I certainly started out this way), try not to get stuck here. Realize that different texts present readers with different opportunities for learning, and that the number of reading engagements required for our students to do some big thinking will vary from text to text. Give yourself permission to allow your little readers the time they need with a text in order for their thinking to evolve and for them to be able to appreciate a book or article with full understanding.

■ Text-Dependent Questions

The second pillar of close reading is text-dependent questions. Questions ranging from the literal to the inferential are sprinkled throughout the multiple readings of a text, allowing students to engage in discussions that help to shape their understanding. These opportunities for collaborative conversations are essential to close reading because they invite students to think about a text in multiple ways as they learn to support their thinking with text evidence. Text-centered discussions often lead students toward an understanding that reaches beyond the book, article, or piece of text being read. For example, as my first-grade students discussed animal movement, their thinking stretched from simply the information in the article to include accounts of their experiences—what they'd seen animals do—and other tidbits from their schema to help each other improve their understanding and make connections with the text.

The great thing about questioning and discussion is that even our primary-grade readers can participate: They do not need to be able to read or write independently in order to engage in thinking about a text. With our guidance and support, students learn to respond to the kinds of questions asked of close readers and to support their ideas with evidence from the text. Examples of these questions include: How do you know? What makes you think that? What clues from the text help you to understand? The chapters that follow provide several ideas for teaching young readers about text-dependent questions and text evidence.

■ Talking, Writing, and Drawing

Earlier in this chapter we explored the writing expectations and independence of older students versus younger students. For K–2 students, speaking and listening opportunities often take the place of written responses in order to provide oral language experiences that support comprehension. However, honoring what students can do, we want to give them the chance to exercise a third pillar of close reading, which involves independently writing or drawing their thinking in some instances. But we must also note that written annotations and reading responses will look different in the primary grades. I often rely on shared or whole-class writing experiences to document K-2 student thinking and response. Allowing students to draw their thinking (see Figure 1.4) is another important way to document immediate thinking about a text and can be a useful indicator of a student's level of comprehension.

■ Noticing and Naming Close Reading

Every time we engage in learning opportunities that involve close reading, it is important to name them as "close reading," so that our students become familiar with the term and begin to associate it with big thinking, conversations, questions, and repeated readings. This is the fourth pillar of close reading. It's almost like we are asking them to switch their thinking caps to deep-thinking mode as we dive into a text together. Our students must know that close reading is a different kind of reading experience, one that will require them to think about a text in new ways and answer questions or participate in discussions that lead to new understandings.

While much of the literacy learning your students engage in may already be inadvertently teaching them to be close and careful readers, chances are they don't know that they are practicing their close reading skills when

Figure 1.4
A first-grade student begins to write and draw her thinking as she listens during a close reading experience.

engaging in these activities. We want them to know that close reading is something that readers do; using the language of close reading helps them understand the ways in which this type of reading differs from all the other reading and writing work they engage in on a daily basis. We can say to them, *Friends, sometimes when we do a lot of thinking about one text, we call it close reading.* It's almost as if we have a magnifying glass and we are zooming in to learn everything we can about a book.

In addition to noticing and naming close reading as such, it is important to also name and teach about the other terms that go hand in hand with close reading. Here I'm talking mainly about the word *text*. I know, can't we just call it a book, article, or whatever else it actually is? Yes, we can, but the word *text* should be used interchangeably so that students become familiar with it. Then by the time they get to third grade, they will be well prepared for their reading discussions. I'm also talking about other terms such as *evidence* and *annotate*. It is easy to assume that our students know what we mean when we use these terms, but, really, they may have no idea. Minilessons teaching about text, evidence, and annotation are crucial if we want our students to understand what close reading is and how or when they engage in it. Subsequent chapters offer ideas for making these often unfamiliar words meaningful for even our youngest readers.

The ideas presented in this chapter highlight some of the ways in which primary-grade close reading differs from the close reading experiences that occur in middle and upper grades. The following table outlines those differences and will help you plan for right now—using the suggestions noted in this chapter—while looking ahead to what students will be able to do as they continue close reading practices in the future.

CLOSE READING DIFFERENCES AT-A-GLANCE		
	PRIMARY GRADES	MIDDLE/UPPER GRADES
Reading	Read-Aloud Shared Reading	Independent Reading
Annotation	Teacher-Led Annotating Shared or Guided Annotating Verbal Annotating Annotating with Wikki Stix or Sticky Notes	Independent Annotating "Reading with a Pencil" More In-Depth, Personal Annotating
Reading Response/ Text-Dependent Questions	Written or Drawn Responses Whole-Class or Shared Responses Comprehension Conversations	Written Responses Comprehension Conversations

■ Putting It All Together

Close reading practices, when used appropriately with young readers, have the potential to inspire, engage, and serve as a foundation for further reading and learning to take place. By shifting our mind-set from thinking of close reading as an "extra activity" to seeing it as an all-encompassing reading experience, we make it an essential component of early literacy instruction. Close reading can include many other aspects of reading instruction that are the heart and soul of the early years of school. Rather than causing your literacy instruction to burst at the seams, close reading can be the seam that holds your literacy instruction together and gives it a place and a purpose.

In an era of higher standards, our students need to be exposed to texts that will open their minds, allowing them to showcase all their big thinking. Working alongside our young readers, we are able to help uncover their ideas and wonderings as they apply their literacy learning and schema to a text or topic. If we don't start providing opportunities for deep, text-centered thinking in the primary-grade years, we are waiting too long.

2

Getting Started: Setting Yourself and Your Students Up for Close Reading Success

Just make a mark and see where it takes you.
——PETER H. REYNOLDS, *THE DOT*

If you began your close reading journey like I did, then you know it can feel like just another thing to fit into an already jam-packed schedule. Sure, I can squeeze a close reading experience right in between this mandatory block of time and that other mandatory block of time, this parent email and—oh, wait, is that crying I hear? Of course it is! And don't you dare plan for close reading at this time because so-and-so absolutely needs to pull four kids out for small group! Sound familiar?

It is precisely this craziness of scheduling that led my first close reading attempts to be glorified monologues, where my wiggly students sat (read: sprawled) and watched my performance, not really understanding the point of what I was doing and constantly raising their hands, because Mrs. Stewart, it's an emergency. I did some of my best annotating, thinking aloud, writing, and finding evidence—award-winning, really. But that's just it—I was doing all the work. I was exhausted and my students were bored. Thankfully, these words from *Falling in Love with Close Reading* inspired me to make a change: "Close reading is something we should teach students to do, rather than something we just do to them" (Lehman and Roberts 2014, 4). I realized I was doing the close reading for my students, not teaching them to do it. No wonder I was so frustrated.

The pressure to get kids reading by the end of the year if you are a kindergarten teacher or, if you teach other primary grades, to continue to move students along as readers, can be overwhelming. In this data-driven world, it can be hard to fathom getting rid of a classroom practice in order to insert close reading experiences for students. Our thinking runs along the lines of, If I have to do close reading with my students, then we will not have time for phonemic awareness or guided reading, and my students need phonemic awareness and guided reading. My advice is let's get away from this-or-that instruction. Rather, let's be smart about close reading and implement practices little by little so our young readers can have more "think time" with the same text. The best close reading experiences are embedded in the content you are already teaching and the books you are already reading.

It can be easy as primary-grade teachers to dismiss the idea of close reading as "not developmentally appropriate for my students." We can become so focused on decoding and word work that critical thinking and examination of a text fall by the wayside. The truth is, if we do not plan meaningful opportunities for even our youngest readers to engage deeply with texts, our students are missing out on forming strong connections with authors and their works—connections that can transfer from one reading experience to the next.

The important thing to remember about close reading is that it does not happen overnight. Your little readers are not going to engage in one deeper reading activity and then be miraculously transformed into perfect close readers. And really, that is not the goal anyway. The goal should be supporting students as they (and you) dip a toe into the practices of close reading and guiding them as those practices become part of your reading routine together. Keeping in mind that close reading at the primary-grade level is often a shared experience, the ideas that follow will ease implementation of close reading with your young readers.

■ Sing, Sing a Song

I am far from being the world's greatest singer, but I have found that incorporating music and song into lessons and activities tends to up the engagement factor for young students. Starting each close reading experience with a song frames the learning for my readers; they know that this is a special kind of reading we are going to be doing (although all reading is special in my book!), and that it is their job to help us experience success together. Plus, who doesn't love a good song to get a lesson started? Here are two of my favorite close reading songs that the kids love to sing.

Song No. 1 (Tune: "Alice the Camel")

Part I: Good to use when preparing for a close reading experience.

Let's get ready to CLOSE READ.
We're going to do a CLOSE READ.
Let's get ready to CLOSE READ.
We READ, THINK, and WRITE.
Boom! Boom! Boom! Boom!

Part II: Good to use when you want students to find evidence to support their thinking.

Let's search for the EVIDENCE.
Evidence supports our THINKING.
Pictures and words show the EVIDENCE.
It shows HOW WE KNOW.
Boom! Boom! Boom! Boom!

Song No. 2 (Tune: "Head, Shoulders, Knees, and Toes")

Close reading means some big, big thinking.
Close reading means some big, big thinking
We notice things and find evidence,
Close reading means some big, big thinking!

■ Reading Like Detectives

The easiest way—and most fun in my opinion—to introduce the idea of close reading is to equate it to the work of detectives. As primary teachers, we can learn a lot from Doug Fisher, Nancy Frey, and Diane Lapp (2011) and their work in *Teaching Students to Read Like Detectives: Comprehending, Analyzing, and Discussing Text*. Although this book is a resource more for teachers of students who are already independent readers, the notion of reading like a detective is one that speaks to primary-grade teachers and, most importantly, is one that our little readers can understand.

As is the case with much of what we do as primary-grade teachers, introducing reading like a detective works better when the teaching is paired with a read-aloud about detectives. Some of my favorite sleuthing stories have allowed my students not only to notice and name what a detective does but also to relate those "jobs" to our reading by answering the question, If these are the things a detective does, what do you think it means to read like a detective? The following table lists some of our favorite detective stories.

BOOKS ABOUT DETECTIVES		
TITLE	AUTHOR/ ILLUSTRATOR(YEAR)	DESCRIPTION
Nate the Great	Marjorie Weinman Sharmat (1972)	Boy detective, Nate, must piece together as many clues as possible to solve the case of Annie's lost picture.
Shark Detective!	Jessica Olien (2015)	A lonely shark dreams of being a great detective.
Lady Pancake and Sir French Toast: The Case of the Stinky Stench	Josh Funk/Brendan Kearney (2017)	Inspector Croissant must get to the bottom of this smelly mystery!
Baby Monkey, Private Eye	Brian Selznick/David Serlin (2018)	Baby Monkey is a detective that can crack any case that needs solving!
Detective LaRue: Letters from the Investigation	Mark Teague (2004)	Ike the dog escapes from pet jail in order to take a police investigation into his own hands.

Grandpa's Teeth	Rod Clement (1997)	The whole town is thrown into a tizzy after Grandpa's teeth go missing. The culprit must be found before it's too late!
Ace Lacewing: Bug Detective	David Biedrzycki (2008)	Trusty detective Ace Lacewing must solve the case when Quee- nie Bee goes missing.
Murilla Gorilla, Jungle Detective	Jennifer Lloyd/Jacqui Lee (2013)	Murilla is a bit of a disorganized detective, but when Ms. Chim- panzee's muffins are stolen, she is counting on Murilla to solve the case!
Pipsie, Nature Detective: The Lunchnapper	Rick DeDonato/Tracy Bishop (2016)	While on a school field trip, Pipsie and her turtle friend, Alfred, search for the thief who stole their missing lunches.

When introducing detective work with a story, we sometimes read and discuss the whole book, while other times, like with *Nate the Great*, I simply choose a piece of the book that highlights the detective work I want students to notice the character doing. Either way, use your teacher magic to make a huge deal out of how important and special detectives are. The more you can foster slack-jawed excitement, the better!

Let's take a look at the example of *Nate the Great* (Sharmat 1972), a beginning-reader chapter book about a boy detective who solves mysteries for friends in need. After a brief yet engaging book talk that introduces Nate and the mystery at hand, students enjoy a read-aloud of just a few pages purposefully chosen for their emphasis on the process of detective work. I like to use the opening pages, typically pages 7–23. These pages give enough of an overview of Nate's job as a detective that students are able to start forming or adding to their thinking about detectives. After reading, I ask them to share what kinds of things Nate does that detectives also do. We begin creating a chart together that shows our thinking about detectives (see Figure 2.1).

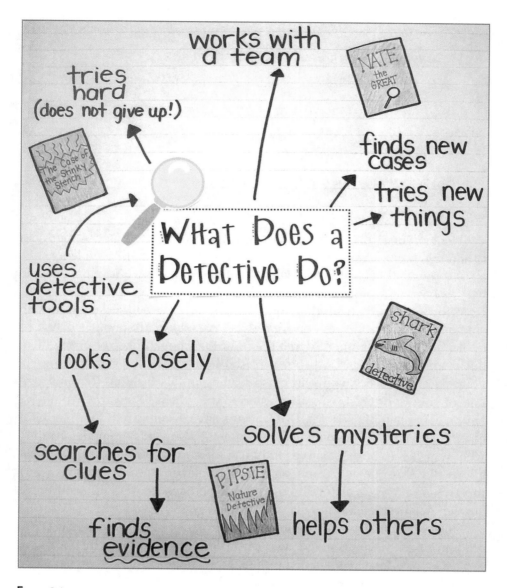

Figure 2.1
Learning about what a detective does helps students understand what it means to read like a detective.

Similarly, a slow picture-walk through any of the books in the *Pipsie, Nature Detective* series will lend itself well to learning what a detective does. As you walk students through the illustrations and talk about the events of the story, pause at times to allow students to reflect on Pipsie's detective work.

Teacher: What kinds of things does Pipsie do that make her a detective?

Student 1: She is always looking for clues.

T: You're right! I noticed that too. What else?

S1: She has a detective bag with detective stuff in it.

T: Oh! Great thinking! Did anyone else notice that? What kinds of things were in her detective bag?

Student 2: She had a book, a camera, a pencil, a notebook, but not a lunch. She lost that.

The conversation continues like this until we've compiled some ideas to add to our chart about what detectives do. When I feel like students have a solid foundational understanding of detective work, we use this chart to help us become reading detectives.

A few pages of a read-aloud or a detailed picture-walk is sometimes all students need to be hooked on *Nate the Great*, *Pipsie*, or another detective book, frantically wanting to grab them for their book boxes or check them out from the library. You'll be surprised how many "mysteries" arise in your classroom when you start close reading in this fashion. Reminiscing, one of my favorite classroom mysteries was, "Mrs. Stewart, I think we have a case on our hands. My Hot Cheetos have disappeared! I will look for clues." This kind of dialogue lets me know that students are understanding what it means to be a detective, and I can refer to authentic classroom situations like this one as I teach students to look for clues in the words and pictures of a text. It also reminds me that perhaps it's time to send home another healthy snack reminder.

Once students have a handle on what a detective does, the transfer to reading takes place. Together, we fill a new chart (see Figure 2.2) with things we can do as readers that mimic the work detectives do, again using the guiding question, We know what a detective does, so what would a reading detective do? Most of the time the students are so excited about being reading detectives that they have no trouble coming up with a slew of ideas to fill a chart; however, do not get discouraged if you sometimes have to guide or nudge their thinking a bit to arrive at some meaningful responses. Suggestions, such as find clues and learn more words, pave the way for deeper thinking nudges, such as, look closely at words and discuss picture clues. I try to always revisit the detective characters we've read about in order to connect and transfer their thinking.

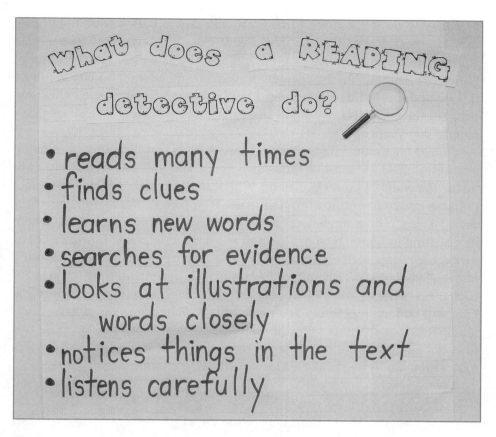

Figure 2.2
Student thinking about what a reading detective can do

As we chart our thinking about being reading detectives, the classroom is abuzz with readers who are ready to dig deeper. Know that this chart you create together is not finite, but can (and will) be added to as you see students trying out new moves as readers or as students think of new ideas for how to read like a detective. This learning and the chart created to house student thinking provide a peek into close reading, energizing young readers and providing them with a context for the work they will be doing.

■ Materials

Primary-grade classrooms are already filled with "stuff." We have even more stuff than our intermediate counterparts because, more often than not, we are responsible for building background knowledge, and sometimes the best way to do that is with stuff. From spices you have carted in because they are used in a part of the world your class is studying, to every math manipulative under the sun, we have it all. And if we are really on top of things, we can tell you the cabinet, drawer, closet, or shelf on which to find it. I do not think of it as hoarding; I think of it as very strategic collecting. I just never know when I might need that pack of colorful feathers that I bought five years ago!

One of the things I love about close reading is that it requires a minimal amount of stuff. At least, it requires nothing that you do not already have inside the walls of your classroom. With that being said, one of my nonnegotiable materials is a magnifying glass. If you're lucky, there is an abandoned science kit somewhere in the scary, dark storage closet at school just waiting to be relieved of its set of magnifying glasses. If you're not as lucky, they are relatively inexpensive to purchase. Whether you choose a larger, "whole-class" magnifying glass or smaller magnifying glasses for each class member, the tool works to signal your young readers' brains that they will be looking closely at a piece of text. With some procedural front-loading of expectations with the individual magnifying glasses (i.e., this does not go in your mouth, up your nose, etc.), students are able to keep this tool with them throughout the close reading experience (see Figure 2.3).

Figure 2.3
Kindergartners excited about close reading

Other materials that you might find useful include highlighters, crayons, pencils, clipboards, and sticky notes. After reading this book you will most likely have a better idea of what materials will work for your purposes.

■ What Is a Text?

An important initial step in teaching young students how to become close, careful readers is to introduce them to the word *text*. We use it all the time when we're close reading with students, but do we really ever teach them what it means? I'm thinking probably not. I surely never did until I realized my students had no idea what I was talking about. Thank goodness it's never too late to try something new!

Here's an idea that will equip your readers with an understanding of the word *text*. Gather texts of all kinds and let students explore them in a whole-class circle or together with their table groups. Magazines, one-page articles, comic books, song lyrics, picture books, lists, wordless books, lunch menus, posters, infographics, take-home flyers from the PTA, websites, even screenshots of fake texting conversations all provide examples of different kinds of texts that students encounter every day. Allow time for students to examine the texts you've provided, and invite them to discuss ideas with their peers about what exactly the word *text* means. Create a chart together similar to the one in Figure 2.4 that captures student thinking and defines the word *text* through their eyes.

During instruction, use text alongside book or article or song or whatever kind of text you are using so that students hear the words together and make the connection that you're talking about the same thing. When students understand what a text is, they are more readily able to participate in close reading activities that require them think about what a text says, does, and means. This small teaching move can have big implications for students learning to be close readers.

■ Noticing

Noticing is a big part of the close reading process with young readers. We all have those expert observers in our classes—the ones who never fail to point out that we indeed do not have P.E. today even though it still says so on the schedule. The noticing that takes place during close reading, though, is a little more than just being observant. This kind of noticing must be modeled and taught so that students know how to notice and what kinds of

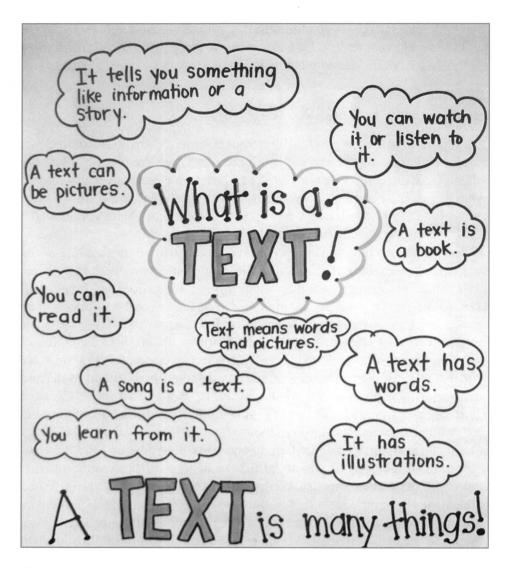

Figure 2.4
Student noticings about different kinds of texts

things warrant noticing. Student noticing lends itself to authentic classroom discussion about how what we notice as readers contributes to our understanding of a text (see Figure 2.5).

Figure 2.5
Invite students to notice as much as possible when reading together.

My knowledge about the importance of noticing is a product of the work of many literacy experts, including Peter Johnston and Maria Walther, who encourage comprehension through collaborative conversations. Peter Johnston's (2004) important question, What are you noticing? is a gateway to deep thinking during classroom literacy discussions. Noticing not only fosters comprehension of the current text being read but also solidifies that comprehension for use during future reading and writing experiences. As Johnston writes, "Once we start noticing certain things, it is difficult not to notice them again" (11). Walther (2015) empowers students to use their noticings to lead the questioning and discussion that takes place in the classroom. Both of these experts have taught me the importance of using literacy instruction as an opportunity to invite student noticing and collaborative conversation.

Similarly, much of my love for close reading comes from the enthusiasm and professional support of Chris Lehman and Kate Roberts (2014). I had the privilege of hearing Chris Lehman speak about close reading at a conference in Illinois a few years ago, where he talked about what he called a "Zoom-In Card," a tool for students to use when practicing their noticing. This close reading manipulative serves as a viewfinder that allows for close and careful attention to the details of a text as students move it across the page. I loved the idea of this kind of noticing card from the start, but I was unsure how it would transfer to the classroom. I thought, Is there really that much to notice in the books we are reading? The answer is yes. There is that much to notice, and if students are given a tool, they will notice things you never even noticed yourself. Using Chris's idea, in my classroom we call these cards Closer-Look Cards, a name my students came up with. Of all the things I have let my students name over the years, this one was by far the most useful (see Figure 2.6).

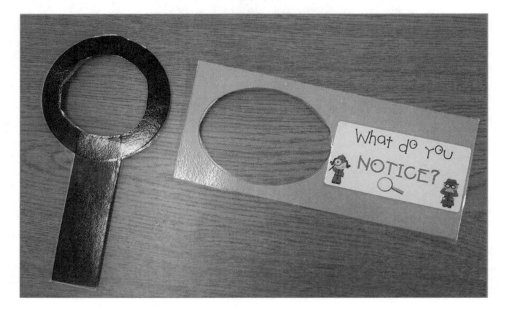

Figure 2.6
Closer-Look Cards support students as they look closely at a text.

The purpose of the Closer-Look Card is for students to get some up-close-and-personal time with books. The idea is that they will slowly slide the viewing space of the card up, down, side to side, and across the pages of a book, looking for things that help them understand the story or information better (see Figure 2.7). Modeling comes into play here. Students are not just going to be able to magically do this on their own. Rather, they will need you to show them how you use the Closer-Look Card. Think aloud for students as you model how to notice and the kinds of things worth noticing in a book, and they will follow your lead. In my experience, a tool such as this works best when the illustrations tell pieces of the story. While young readers can, of course, notice things about the words in a story, the tool encourages attention to those subtle illustration clues as well. Wordless books are great for noticing! It is also important to note that the card is a scaffold that can be slowly removed as students show they can notice just as well without it.

Figure 2.7
Model and think aloud when introducing students to the Closer-Look Cards. Allow them to hear and see how you notice.

Time with the Closer-Look Card is maximized if students use it after a text has been read aloud at least once. This way, they are more apt to notice things that contribute to the story or topic rather than just random things. However, students do use the cards with their independent reading books as well. Because even our youngest readers can notice, learning is maximized when students are able to keep the Closer-Look Cards in their book bins for use during independent and partner reading time. The more they are able to practice, the better they will be at noticing things that help them think critically or uniquely about the text. Again, showing students how you notice things and how the things you notice shape your understanding of a text is crucial to their being able to do it on their own.

The Closer-Look Cards are quick and easy to make, and you won't go overboard on your copy and print limit (for those of us working under paper and color ink restrictions—cough, cough, me). All you need is card stock or construction paper and a pair of scissors to get these things up and running in your classrooms. Cut the card stock into the shape of a rectangle, and then cut a "viewing space" somewhere out of the middle so that students can see through it. Once you've got the cards made, students decorate them using markers, crayons, stickers, and so on, giving them ownership of the tool and (hopefully) more motivation to use it. If the laminator happens to be working that day, the added reinforcement of laminating the cards will give them a longer shelf life, especially for students whose organizational skills include shoving things wherever they will fit and hoping to find them later. I have also made Closer-Look Cards in the shape of magnifying glasses (see Figure 2.8), which the students love. As an added scaffold, a sentence frame (or a few sentence-frame options) can be added to the Closer-Look Card to encourage and support speaking skills. I listen in on the language my students use and really try to follow their lead when suggesting sentence frames. The sentence frame I overhear most often is, simply, "I notice that . . . ," but students have also come up with "I can see

Figure 2.8
Kindergarten students use their Closer-Look Cards to notice new things in *Journey* by Aaron Becker.

here that . . . " and "This must mean . . . ," among others. Sentence frames give some students the confidence they need to participate in a classroom conversation about their noticings. Using a sentence frame in conjunction with a Closer-Look Card is also helpful as students learn to write and draw their thinking following an initial reading of a text using a page like the one found in Appendix A.

Listen in on this conversation with a kindergarten student who was using his Closer-Look Card during independent reading with the book *Journey* by Aaron Becker. We had read this book the previous day as a class, and it was flying off the shelves in our classroom and school library so that students could read it using their Closer-Look Cards.

> **Student:** *Mrs. Stewart, I noticed something new I never noticed before!*
>
> **Teacher:** *You did? That's wonderful! Even though you've already read this book, there is still more to notice!*
>
> **S:** *Yeah. I noticed that right here in the girl's room, there is the purple bird really small out the window! And it is even on the next page too—out the window again!*
>
> **T:** *Wow! That is something that I did not notice when I was reading. Why do you think Aaron Becker put that bird there? Why did he made it so small?*
>
> **S:** *I think that he put it there because he wanted us to know that the bird was going to be part of the story. Maybe it is small so that only good noticers could find it.*
>
> **T:** *I think you might be right about that. Let's remember to share this with our friends at the end of workshop time today.*

This is just one of the many conversations that could take place in your classroom as a result of teaching kids how to notice as they read and providing them with a tool to do so.

The following table provides a list of books that will serve as a launching point for incorporating and embedding the idea of noticing into your reading instruction. Not all books or texts that you will use for close reading will lend themselves to using the Closer-Look Card. That's okay. Once students are familiar with how and what to notice, they can really take ownership of the card and of their noticing, doing it without your prompting and with books of their choosing. Remember, the purpose of noticing is to look closely and deeply at a text in order to shape understanding and form new thinking. Students can learn to do this both inside and outside a close reading experience.

BOOKS THAT INVITE NOTICING		
TITLE	AUTHOR/ ILLUSTRATOR (YEAR)	DESCRIPTION
One Day, The End: Short, Very Short, Shorter-Than-Ever Stories	Rebecca Kai Dotlich/ Fred Koehler (2015)	A young girl tells her story in short, sweet sentences, but the real story is waiting in the illustrations.
Sidewalk Flowers	JonArno Lawson/Sydney Smith (2015)	This wordless book follows a young girl who collects flowers and gives them as gifts while on a walk with her too-busy father.
Journey	Aaron Becker (2013)	A mysterious red crayon leads a girl on an unforgettable magical journey.
The Sound of Silence	Katrina Goldsaito/ Julia Kuo (2016)	Yoshio journeys through his busy city in Japan in search of the most beautiful sound.
Snappsy the Alligator: Who Did Not Ask to Be in This Book	Julie Falatko/Tim Miller (2016)	A disgruntled alligator is annoyed at the narrator for following him around and telling his life story.
Giant Squid	Candace Fleming/Eric Rohmann (2016)	This picture book takes readers deep down into the ocean to learn about one of the most mysterious creatures in the world, the giant squid.
Blizzard	John Rocco (2014)	John Rocco tells the true story of his life as a young boy during the Blizzard of 1978.
Mr. Tiger Goes Wild	Peter Brown (2013)	Mr. Tiger is tired of pretending he is not a wild animal.
Looking Closely Through the Forest	Frank Serafini (2014)	Take a close look at things in the forest with this book from Frank Serafini's Looking Closely series.

If you want students to do some noticing on the same text, it is helpful for them to work in pairs or teams of three so they can discuss their ideas with peers (see Figure 2.9). This means you'll need to buy some Starbucks for the librarian, whom you will have to ask to find you several copies of the same text. The great thing about noticing, though, is that students can also do it independently. They need not all be noticing with the same book. Consider using the Closer-Look Cards in a read-around (Layne 2009) scenario or during independent or partner reading. My students keep their cards in their book bins for easy access and quick practice.

Figure 2.9
Kindergarten students practice being expert observers during reading workshop.

Affirming and honoring something a young reader has noticed is a powerful way to positively impact his or her reading life. Furthermore, practicing the art of noticing independently provides a feeling of empowerment and ownership that will light up any reader's face. Again, learning is maximized when student noticings are shared and used to develop new understandings.

■ Annotating with Little Readers and Writers

Before you let the words *annotate* and *primary-grade students* in the same sentence cause a rise in your stress level, I am here as living proof that it can be done. Not only can it be done, but it can be done without tears (from students or teachers!). Let's begin by taking a closer look (no pun intended) at the definition of the word *annotate*, which, according to dictionary.com, means "to add notes to a text giving explanation or comment." Okay, great. Good to know. Now what?

We do as we have always done as primary-grade teachers, which is figure out how to make this work for our young readers and, since annotation by definition requires some form of writing, our young writers. The heart and soul of annotation is the reader tracking his or her thinking throughout the reading of a text. This can be done in several ways, but it begins with building an understanding of what annotating is and why it is important.

When I think of annotating, I am immediately reminded of a late September day when my students waltzed outside for recess following a particularly lengthy rainfall. Around twenty minutes later, they returned—out of breath, a little sweaty, and ready to tackle the rest of the day. And then I saw Kevin, traipsing into the classroom behind all the others with an outrageous amount of mud caked onto his gym shoes. Now, I'm pretty sure I cautioned everyone to try to avoid the mud, but it appeared upon seeing Kevin that my wording could have been a bit clearer. His muddy tracks created a trail from the school doors all the way down the hallway to our classroom door. He looked up at me with knowing eyes and said, "Ummm, I think I need to go clean my shoes off." Bravo for problem solving, Kevin, even if it was just a little too late.

Annotation is a lot like Kevin's muddy trail from that fall day. It helps us keep track of where we came from, where we are now, and where we are going next as readers. Kevin's footprints let us know where he was, and we could visibly see the path he took to get to his destination. The same is true for our annotations as readers—they mark the path our thinking takes as we work through a text.

A story like Kevin's helps when introducing a tricky skill such as annotation, but sometimes, even in the unpredictable primary-grade world, the perfect story does not always fall into our laps at the perfect time. Luckily, there are books to help. I often approach the task of introducing annotation to my early and emergent readers in the best way I know how—with a picture book. The book *Tracks in the Snow* by Wong Herbert Yee (see Figure 2.10) is perfect for beginning a conversation about leaving "tracks" as a reader. Ideally, this book works best if students have some prior experience with playing in the snow, but it might work regardless if you can get creative with your delivery. I always say that nothing is impossible for a teacher. *Tracks in the Snow* is the story of a young girl who follows some tracks that have been left in the snow outside her home. She is expecting to find a big bear or a fluffy rabbit at the end of the tracks, but when the tracks lead her right back home, she realizes they are actually her own tracks from her walk in the snow the day before.

Figure 2.10
Use the book *Tracks in the Snow* to introduce annotation.

After reading, I teach my students that just like the girl in the story, who leaves tracks that show her walking path, readers leave tracks as they read that show the path of their thinking throughout a text, and those tracks are called annotations. Annotations let us know that a reader was here. A reader has left her tracks—her thinking—on this text. We then immediately chart that learning in order to memorialize this fancy new term, annotating, that we have just learned together. This chart and this vocabulary will stay with us all year long as we continue to leave our tracks on texts we read. In the table that follows, I have included some read-aloud options from which to choose.

PICTURE BOOKS ABOUT LEAVING TRACKS OR FOOTPRINTS		
TITLE	AUTHOR/ ILLUSTRATOR (YEAR)	DESCRIPTION
Tracks in the Snow	Wong Herbert Yee (2003)	A young girl follows tracks that have been left outside her home after a snowfall.
Wild Tracks! A Guide to Nature's Footprints	Jim Arnosky (2008)	The information in this book is matched by its powerfully real illustrations of wild animals and their tracks.
Big Tracks, Little Tracks: Following Animal Prints	Millicent E. Selsam/ Marlene Hill Donnelly (1991)	This informational book teaches readers how to identify animal prints and learn something about the animals who leave them.
Nate the Great and the Snowy Trail	Marjorie Weinman Sharmat/Marc Simont (1982)	Nate follows tracks in the snow to help Rosamund find his lost birthday present!
Footprints in the Snow	Mai Matsuoka (2008)	Since all storybook wolves are portrayed as mean and nasty, Wolf sets off to write a story about a nice wolf. He follows footprints in the snow in hopes of making a new friend.

■ Annotating for Different Reasons

Another important point about annotation for students to understand is that we annotate for different reasons. We cannot simply say to our students, Today you are going to annotate. Ready? Go. We must give them a purpose—a reason why we are marking up a text. Sometimes that reason is simply to show and track anything we are thinking while reading. Other times we are annotating in order to locate specific things an author does, to respond to a question, or to form an opinion about something. I share some specific purposes for annotation and ways that students can mark up a text in the sections that follow. When we give students a reason to annotate, and when we model and annotate along with them, it helps to avoid the frustration that often befalls teachers who think, My kids just don't get how to annotate. Regardless of the purpose, when we support young readers in annotating, they learn that annotation is a way for them to keep track of their thoughts as they read or as we read together.

■ Making Annotation Manageable and Meaningful

Annotation seems like a fairly manageable concept, but if we are not careful it can get out of hand fast. In addition to simply noting thoughts and making observations, there is an endless amount of symbols and marks that could be used to annotate a text. When I first began learning about close reading, I saw (and I still see) many different symbols that students must know and use while annotating. Most of us find ourselves teaching these symbols just so we can check off that we "taught" our students to annotate. A question mark means this, and an infinity symbol means that, and an upside-down parakeet with blue feathers means this. My head is spinning just thinking about it! Yes, my students could tell you what each symbol meant, but did it have any meaning for them as readers? My guess is probably not. Sometimes the system gets the best of us all. If we truly examine why we use these symbols and whether they are helping readers connect with text, we might rethink their purpose in our classrooms.

While I do think some annotating symbols are okay, I caution against their overuse and their use without support. Sure, it is great for students to know that a question mark can be used when they have a question about something, but isn't it much more beneficial if they actually write or talk about what that question is? If you are going to use annotation symbols, make sure they are meaningful. Meaningful means more than just introducing and reviewing standard annotation symbols until students start to use them. Meaningful means that the annotations matter to students.

One way to model annotations is to create them during authentic reading experiences with your students rather than just telling them what they mean and where to put them. For example, during a read-aloud or shared reading experience you might think aloud about the importance of a specific sentence or two. *Friends, I think that this sentence is really important because it shows the point in the story where Sally takes action. How do you think I could mark this to show my thinking? What is a good way to show that something we are reading is important?* Students might respond with ideas such as circling the sentence, putting a star by it, or marking it with an exclamation point, and then you have an authentically created annotation symbol for your students to use.

By inviting students to have a say in the way they mark up a text, you are not only modeling that reading is thinking but also honoring their ability to make decisions about their learning. Also, start small and end small. It is better for students to use one or two annotation symbols with meaning and understanding than it is for them to have three anchor charts worth of symbols from which to choose and limited opportunities to make sense of any of them.

The same goes for all those different-color highlighters we are asking students to use, where each color means a different thing. By the time the students have finished annotating, their highlighting has blended into an unpleasing brownish color and their papers have holes in them where the ink has bled through.

■ Emergent Reader Annotations

Like symbols, highlighting is another great practice that we can misuse or overuse if we are not careful. The following are a few symbol-free and highlighter-free annotation ideas to use with your primary-grade readers.

■ Search and Find

One of the first annotation methods I show my students involves using decoding skills we are already working on and with which students are already familiar. I mentioned earlier in this chapter that the more you can transfer and apply the learning students are already doing, the more meaningful your instruction will be, not only in terms of close reading but also in other literacy events in your classroom. Annotating can spring from the phonemic awareness, phonics, or high-frequency word work that is already part of your students' reading and writing experience. "Marking up" a text is easier for students if they are looking for something concrete that they are learning or have already learned. I call these search and find annotations because students are searching for something in the text and (hopefully) finding it.

Let's say we have been working on letter-sound relationships. I might ask students to find and circle (or highlight, or color) all the words from the text that begin with the /b/ sound. Watching them annotate and examining their annotations provides me with information not only about their awareness of the /b/ sound in relation to the letter b but also about possible b and d confusion, and even their level of understanding of the difference between a letter and a word.

Another example might be words with –*ed* endings, a tricky two-letter combination that can make any teacher curse the English language. By asking students to find and annotate words that have –*ed* endings, we allow them the opportunity to notice for themselves that an –*ed* at the end of the word can make different sounds, and we can guide them as they discover similarities and differences between the words they found. This is so much more powerful than a stand-and-deliver lesson about the three sounds of – *ed* (cue *Peanuts*' teacher's wah wah voice) using decontextualized words. Annotation in this form requires that students take a closer look at the words they are reading in order to form new understandings about letter and word relationships (see Figure 2.11).

Search and find annotating works really well with Big Books because you can mark up a text as a class, but if you share my love-hate relationship with Big Books, then you know it is not always practical to use them. I recommend using a document camera, interactive whiteboard, or iPad on which you can mark up the text digitally, or consider adapting (with

Figure 2.11
Students digitally annotate words with –ed endings.

permission, of course) a page or section of a book to distribute for students use. Wikki Stix®, pieces of wax-covered yarn that definitely make you wonder *Why didn't I think of that?*, are great for this kind of annotating because they are removable and replaceable—not to mention motivating for students (see Figure 2.12). Simply cut the Wikki Stix to the size needed and use them to mark up letters, words, sentences, illustrations, or other parts of the text worth noting that match your purpose for reading. Highlighter tape also works well if you can remember to remove it after reading so as to not open the book a year later only to find that same highlighter tape has literally been cemented onto the page. (Please tell me this does not just happen to me.) As far as materials go, like anything in teaching, find what works for you and go with it.

Sometimes we play on the swings but by the middle of winter the snow gets so deep there's no room for our legs! We have to throw the swing over the top to make the chains shorter. And the teeter-totters usually freeze to the ground. Bang! Bang! Bang! We have to kick them over and over again to break off the ice. Before anyone goes down the slide it is covered with ice crystals that sparkle like glitter. It's like sliding down a glacier.

Figure 2.12
Wikki Stix are great for whole-group annotations. Here, students used them to mark words with beginning consonant blends.

After we have practiced together several times across different reading experiences, students have the opportunity to practice annotating their own books during independent reading. I typically give them two full Wikki

Stix and a pair of scissors that they keep in their book boxes to cut and use over and over again for annotating. This adds another layer of independence to their close reading process. I often give individual students a focus for their independent annotations (for example, Melanie needs more practice with – ed endings, so she uses her Wikki Stix to annotate and look closer at words with –ed endings), but I also allow them the freedom to come up with their own reasons for annotating. During reading conferences or small-group instruction, it is fun to see how students take this simple practice of marking up a text and make it their own. I use this information about students' annotation practices to inform my next instructional moves with them.

You may need to work with students to set some necessary parameters around what good search and find annotation looks like. For example, you might have a student like Mara, who used more than her fair share of Wikki Stix in her Big Book because "I am searching and finding every letter, Mrs. Stewart!" Insert face-palm emoji here, right? Yes indeed, Mara was annotating all the letters. As far as using time wisely goes, this was not one of our brightest moments. Luckily, I caught Mara before she completely depleted us of Wikki Stix and—because one of her goals at the time was understanding the concepts of a letter, word, and sentence—challenged her to find just the first letter of each word. A few annotation guidelines here and there can make your life a lot easier.

■ Share Your Thinking

As mentioned earlier in this chapter, annotation is a way for students and teachers alike to keep track of their thinking about a text. For primary-grade teachers, it can be challenging to teach our students that reading is thinking, and even more challenging to ask them to think about their thinking. Thankfully, we have the work of Debbie Miller to teach us how to maximize thinking time in our classrooms. Much of my students' ability to understand and cultivate their thinking comes from her work. Once a classroom community of "rigor, inquiry, and intimacy" (Miller 2012, 21) is created, deep thinking can take place.

Share Your Thinking is a learning activity that comes early in the close reading process in my classroom, but it can be revisited throughout a close reading sequence of lessons if desired. The idea is pretty straightforward. Following reading, I ask students to share, by writing and/or drawing in their reader's notebooks, what they are thinking now that they have heard the text. Here is an example. After our first reading of *The Snowy Day* by

Ezra Jack Keats, I invited students to share their thinking by first sharing mine. In my notebook I drew, as students watched, a picture of Peter feeling sad that his snowball had melted, and I wrote, I am thinking about Peter's snowball. He was sad. I explained my thinking to students and then asked them to draw or write some thinking of their own. Some of them simply drew pictures, while others wrote some sentences about things that had happened to Peter on his adventure in the snow (see Figure 2.13). Examining each student's thinking and listening in as each explains their rationale allows me to form a quick assessment as to whether students have gotten the gist of the story. Remember to honor each student's thinking, even if it mimics ours, because some students need to stand on our shoulders until they are ready to fly on their own.

Figure 2.13
This student's Share Your Thinking page shows his lingering thoughts after a first reading of *The Snowy Day*.

Sometimes it is best to see what students come up with in terms of their writing, while other times a sentence frame like I am thinking . . . or Reading this makes me think that . . . might guide their thinking in a meaningful direction. Either way, students will have documented their thinking about a text, which will serve as a launching point for rich discussion throughout the rest of the close reading sequence. A Share Your Thinking page with space for students to write (on the lines) and/or draw (in the circle) their initial thoughts about a text is included in Appendix A.

SHARE YOUR THINKING SENTENCE FRAMES

- I am thinking . . .

- I wonder . . .

- Reading this makes me think . . .

- After reading this, I think . . .

- I liked/disliked . . . because . . .

- I noticed . . .

- I have a question about . . .

- After reading this, I am feeling . . . because . . .

■ Leave a Thinking Trail

Similar to the Share Your Thinking activity, pausing periodically and purposefully throughout reading to allow students to draw or write their thinking is a great way for them to see the path their thinking takes throughout the text. We call this a "thinking trail" because students are able to see how their/our thinking changed, evolved, or remained the same throughout the reading of a text. I use the terms *periodically* and *purposefully* because I have found that with primary-grade readers, it works best to plan checkpoints, or think points as we call them, at which students can express their thinking while reflecting on the meaning of the text.

The thinking trail (see Figures 2.14 and 2.15) begins as a teacher-modeled experience, then becomes a shared experience until students are able to give it a try independently. Often by the time students get to try it on their own, they are bursting with excitement, which, I tell myself, is more than just because they get to use a clipboard while we read. As a person with what some might call an unhealthy obsession with office supplies, I totally get the kids' excitement.

Figure 2.14
Plenty of group reading experiences with teacher-modeled think-alouds will support students before they begin to record their own thinking.

Figure 2.15
A first grader's completed thinking trail for
The Smallest Girl in the Smallest Grade

Sometimes it is helpful to give students a focus for their thinking trail. For example, if students are learning about how predictions help them check their understanding as they read, the think points might have a predicting focus. Or, if studying characters, you might want students to keep track of a character's actions or feelings throughout a text. Most often, however, I want to see what the text means to each student, so I try to limit the restrictions in terms of what they can and cannot include on their thinking trails. After all, it is their thinking. I am simply the facilitator. Figure 2.16 shows an example of a completed whole-group thinking trail for the text *Yard Sale* by Eve Bunting.

Student pages for the thinking trail are included in the appendices. Appendix B provides a thinking trail with space for students to draw and write their thinking, while the thinking trail included in Appendix C is

Figure 2.16

A completed thinking trail for the book *Yard Sale* by Eve Bunting shows the changes in character and mood that students noticed throughout the story.

solely for drawn responses. Both documents will allow students to independently track their thinking throughout a close reading experience.

■ Sharing Annotations

The importance of peer sharing cannot be overlooked in any subject area, and close reading is no different. As students learn to annotate across different types of texts and for different reasons, be sure to provide ways for them to share their annotations and their thinking with others. Sharing their work allows students the opportunity not only to show their annotations to others but also to articulate and explain the way they have marked up the text. As they share, students get ideas from one another and construct new thinking (see Figure 2.17).

Sharing can become time-consuming, but there are ways to share quickly and easily. For example, students can take a photo of their annotations and post it to a digital portfolio app, like Seesaw, where they can record themselves speaking about their process. You can also print photos of student annotations and display them in your classroom (if you can evade the ever-vigilant printer police). A thirty-second peer share at the end

Figure 2.17
Two students share their thinking using the annotations they made while listening to a text.

of reading workshop is another good go-to if you're pressed for time—and let's be honest, you are pressed for time.

■ Guiding Principles of Annotation with Young Readers and Writers

The following table contains some guidelines to anchor your annotation work with your little readers and writers. Let these principles serve as a launching point as you teach your students how to keep track of their thinking about a text.

ANNOTATING WITH PRIMARY STUDENTS —GUIDING PRINCIPLES
• Remember that much close reading in the primary grades is a shared experience between teacher and students, and annotations are no different. Often we will track our thinking as a class, annotating together and discussing how those annotations help us as readers.
• Think about using annotation as a way to incorporate, transfer, and apply learning that is already taking place in the classroom.
• If writing words or sentences proves to be challenging, remember to honor drawing as a form of writing. Big thinking can come out through drawing, so we must not discount this mode of expression.
• Along with the reader's thinking, the text is the focus during close reading. If the annotations become a point of struggle for students, the focus will shift from the text to the annotating. Try to keep the text and the thinking as the focus by honoring what students can do.
• Since it is not typically possible for each student to have a copy of a text, consider alternate forms of annotation, such as digital annotations using a device.
• Always allow time for students to share their annotations and their thinking with their peers. When students discuss their ideas and hear the ideas of others, they learn to form new, text-based understandings.

■ Finding Evidence

When introducing the notion of text evidence to little readers, recall the detective analogy from the beginning of this chapter. Remind students that a detective could not solve a case without having some kind of evidence to prove that her thinking was correct. Most students have heard the term *evidence* from some Saturday-morning cartoon, but it is helpful to give this term a place in your classroom learning environment by naming and defining it together. Inviting students to share their input and write on any of the anchor charts or learning visuals that will fill the walls of your classroom gives them a greater sense of ownership of the content—it lets them know that this is our learning, not just yours. When we define terms together and post them in the classroom for reference, they naturally become a part of our learning vocabulary. Figure 2.18 depicts a chart I use in my classroom when learning about text evidence.

Introducing young readers to the concept of evidence and also conveying its importance is no small undertaking. Even for older students, the idea of going back into a text to pick out information that will help support their thinking is a mountain of a task that requires engagement, relevance, and

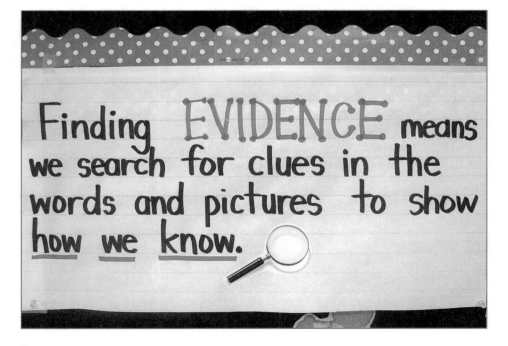

Figure 2.18
This chart helps students remember what evidence is and how readers use it to understand a text.

stamina. While we cannot fully climb that mountain with our little readers, we can start them off on their journey with the right tools to make it to the top.

Beginning with the basic evidential question, How do you know? we are able to ease early readers into the process of supporting their thinking with evidence from the text. This familiar question provides the foundation on which understanding is built. We ask students this question all the time throughout their literacy learning, not only during read-aloud and shared reading but also when we confer with them or meet for literacy learning in small groups.

An easy way to introduce and practice this question is (surprise!) with a picture book. Olivier Tallec's *Who What Where?* and its predecessor, *Who Done It?* are a primary-grade teacher's dream for teaching the concept of evidence. Not only that, they are also student favorites that will be loved so much you'll have to buy new copies each year—there are only so many trips to the book hospital that a little hardcover can take! In addition to being great for close reading, *Who What Where?* and *Who Done It?* are also great for enticing struggling or reluctant writers. Encourage your young writers to try their hand at drawing some evidence as they create a similar book in writing workshop!

Both of Tallec's creative picture books follow a simple question-and-answer format. On each page a question is posed about one of the characters in the illustration, and readers are required to closely scan this cast of characters to find out which one of them answers the question. For example, one of the first pages of *Who Done It?* reads, "Who played with that mean cat?" With ten characters to choose from who all look different and are doing different things, young readers have to search and notice the one character with scratches all over her body and a not-so-happy face. Once students have "cracked the case" by finding the character who answers the question, we turn our attention to the evidence. How do we know that this is the character who played with the mean cat? What is our evidence?

When we introduce evidence to students in this way, they are practicing a complicated idea in a not-so-complicated manner. You will notice I am not asking them to write their answers using a formulaic response, like I know this because . . . or In the text it says . . . Rather, we are starting the conversation by defending our thinking, providing students with Britton's "sea of talk" (1970, 164) that fosters their literacy development. The importance of discussion and dialogue in the classroom gives us permission to share the experience of finding evidence with students, remembering that much of close reading in the primary grades is a shared or whole-class experience. We should not be asking students who cannot yet read the words on the page to find, highlight, and write text evidence. In the chapters that follow, finding evidence with little readers is revisited as we explore what this looks like in a close reading experience.

Getting the idea of finding evidence to stick in little readers' minds involves naming it when it happens naturally in the classroom. Consider the following exchange between a kindergarten student and teacher.

> *Student: Mrs. Stewart, how do you know when it is time for us to go to recess?*
>
> *Teacher: How do I know? I think you are asking me to provide you with evidence! Let me show you my evidence for how I know when it is time for you to go to recess.* [Retrieves school recess schedule and points to the evidence of the kindergarten recess time.]

I've included this exchange to highlight the types of conversations that happen all the time in our classrooms and to allow us to think about how our responses to students can become more purposeful. While it may seem like a stretch to be able to respond in such a way to everything that students bring forth (especially when we can barely get in a word sometimes!), when the opportunity presents itself we must seize it. A conversation such as this not only reinforces the learning taking place in the classroom but also provides a real-world context for the vocabulary that goes hand in hand with close reading.

Consider this exchange that took place during a reading conference with a second grader, who was reading *The World According to Humphrey* by Betty G. Birney.

> *Teacher: What are you noticing about Humphrey now that you are a little bit further into this book?*
>
> *Student: Well right now I am noticing that Humphrey is learning a lot of things. Like he is very curious.*
>
> *T: It is interesting that you noticed Humphrey's curiosity. What evidence tells you that he is curious? What types of things does he do that make you think he is curious?*

S: Like when he goes to the kids' houses he learns how to do stuff. He learns to read some words and he learns about their stuff because he is curious.

Such conferences or small-group conversations remind students that whole-class literacy learning applies to their individual reading experiences as well. Additionally, they provide mini teaching opportunities to build student confidence and specificity when providing evidence. Following are a few of my favorite go-to books when introducing the notion of text evidence.

GOOD BOOKS FOR ANSWERING HOW DO YOU KNOW?		
TITLE	AUTHOR/ ILLUSTRATOR (YEAR)	DESCRIPTION
Clothesline Clues to Jobs People Do	Kathryn Heling and Deborah Hembrook/ Andy Robert Davies (2012)	Given an illustrated set of clothing that belongs to a certain profession, readers must gather clues from the pictures and words to determine whose clothes they are.
Who Done It?	Olivier Tallec (2015)	Readers are asked a question about a cast of characters on each page. They must use clues from the details in each characters depiction in order to answer each question correctly.
Who What Where?	Olivier Tallec (2016)	This follow-up to *Who Done It?* revisits that same cast of characters, this time with more challenging questions for the reader to answer.
That Is NOT a Good Idea!	Mo Willems (2013)	A hungry fox invites a goose to dinner, but readers know that is NOT a good idea.
Whose Hands Are These? A Community Helper Guessing Book	Miranda Paul/Luci- ana Navarro Powell (2015)	In this guessing book, readers match the community helper to their pair of hands using the tools they need.

■ An Invitation

As you reflect on your students and your classroom, you can probably already think of books or learning opportunities you provide that would lend themselves to some of the ideas outlined in this chapter. By embedding the elements of close reading into the reading experiences that are already taking place, you can maximize student thinking and encourage them to revisit a loved book through a different lens or with a different purpose. Reading, writing, speaking, and listening are things we do each day with our students. Close reading challenges students to put these everyday skills to work as they dig deeper and form new understandings.

When we start small and close to home (with what our readers can do), the desired result does not seem so far away. The introductory elements outlined in this chapter will pave the way for meaningful close reading opportunities to take place in the classroom with your young readers. Give some of these ideas a try, and you might be surprised with the capability of even your littlest readers. When we make close reading more accessible to primary students, it becomes one less thing to "squeeze in" and one more thing that contributes to a classroom community of joyful readers.

3

Moving Forward: Digging Deeper with Young Readers

Then everyone began to sing,
"Yes, readers can do anything!"
—JUDY SIERRA, *BORN TO READ*

Now that we've got an understanding of some foundational elements of close reading with young readers, we can move into what close reading actually looks like in practice in a primary classroom. Just as our mentors Doug Fisher, Nancy Frey, and Diane Lapp (2011) remind us, students are not going to be able to develop these reading habits on their own. We teachers must expertly craft reading opportunities that will support our students as they learn to engage in text-centered critical thinking and discussion. Creating these opportunities, like anything relating to close reading with early or emergent readers, can be intimidating or seem overwhelming. This chapter explores ways in which teachers can support the development of close and critical readers without losing sight of our students' developmental reading abilities and, most importantly, while keeping the joy of reading at the forefront of our instruction.

■ Capitalizing on the Love of Reading

What many of us enjoy most about teaching students in their early years is that they get excited about almost anything. For the most part, they love school. They love their teachers, their friends, and reading. Many primary-grade students are self-motivated to dive into the classroom library (literally, there's diving, especially if it's Friday afternoon) and curl up with some of their favorite books. If we've done our jobs, our students know at least a few authors and illustrators by name and can easily rattle off their favorite book characters or topics about which to read.

Whether students are being read to or they are the ones doing the reading, interacting with books brings them joy. Their faces light up during an aha moment while reading John Rocco's *Blackout*; their bodies howl with laughter after yet another hilarious reader in Mo Willems's Elephant and Piggie series; tears stream down their faces after hearing *Each Kindness* by Jacqueline Woodson. The reading experiences we provide for our young students will shape the readers they are to become in the future.

How do we ensure that these reading experiences will lay enough of a foundation to keep our students reading for years to come? Two ways are by providing as many reading experiences as possible and by varying the kinds of interactions students have with texts. This is where close reading comes into play; we capitalize on our students' love of reading and on their interests by guiding them to think critically and creatively about the topics those texts present.

Now, I know what you're thinking. *Close reading* and *love* are words that cannot possibly be connected in any way, shape, or form. I think this is because we have unconsciously conditioned ourselves—and, in turn, our students—to believe that close reading is hard, meaningless, and absolutely zero fun. And who can blame us when the terms *close reading*, *complex texts*, *evidence*, and *rigor* were thrown at us with little else other than to say they were all now required in our instruction? I think we forgot somewhere in the madness that we teachers (read: superheroes) know our practice and, quite honestly, were already providing many of these reading and learning opportunities for our students before the new shifts came along. We forgot that we love books just as much as our students do. We let our reading joy slip away and shoved close reading into this area in our brains where all the bad things go. All these ideas—complexity, rigor, evidence—were not so scary before we had names for them.

If we change our perspective on close reading from something that we have to do to something that we get to do, we bring the joy back into reading instruction for our students and for ourselves. I am not saying this is easy to do, especially in schools and districts where close reading mandates are strict and heavy. There is only so much enthusiasm you can muster for a practice that you might not yet believe in (even though teachers are really good at enthusiasm). A good place to start building your enthusiasm is to think about what your students—and you—love most about reading. Then think of reading opportunities that will expand these areas of joy, turning them into a shout-from-the-rooftops kind of reading love.

Here's an example from my work with students. Second graders were in the midst of their animal habitats unit, and I was working with a small group of students who were fascinated by the ocean. These kids wanted to read about anything and everything under the sea (pun definitely intended), so I chose the book *Giant Squid* by Candace Fleming (2016), a text that might not be accessible to them if they were reading on their own, but one that without a doubt capitalized on their reading interests at that point in time. I was thrilled to have this close reading experience because my students were so excited about the book and the topic. Rather than struggle through a text that sparked little motivation, I intentionally chose their love of the ocean as a catalyst for close reading.

My goal with *Giant Squid* was to expand this group's love of ocean books while guiding them toward new learning, deeper thinking, and—if I was lucky—some constructive analysis. I started small, building on students' ocean schema and sorting words from the text to learn concepts during a prereading activity. From there, students were invited to take an amazing journey into the depths of the ocean. With support over several days, they collectively noticed and named moves that the author and illustrator made and discussed why those moves were important to the understanding of the text. They expanded and reinforced their vocabulary, linking words in this book to words they had read in other ocean books. They formed their own questions and wonderings, and they used their new learning to form opinions about the mysterious giant squid. Is that close reading? I'd say so.

I knew students had truly read for meaning and understanding when they came away with some solid thinking (The giant squid is huge, yet mysterious.) as well as some wonderings (Are there any other animals that lurk down deep that scientists do not know much about?), which required some further reading and research on their part. There's no better feeling than having five students beg you to buy more copies of a rigorous book that they now have the capacity to read and understand. (See Chapter 5 for a complete lesson sequence for *Giant Squid*.)

With *Giant Squid* I used different approaches that allowed students to experience the text in a variety of ways. We looked at text structure, vocabulary, and inclusion of facts over the course of a few days. By varying our instructional moves, we teach students that there is more than one way to read a book. Close reading with our students should not be something that chips away at their love of reading. Rather, it should add to that love by intentionally connecting with and inspiring the readers in our classrooms.

In addition to capitalizing on topics that students love, we can also weave beloved titles or characters with close reading practices because the engagement is already there. Kids trip over themselves to get to those books in the library. Your challenge, then, during a close reading experience is to provide opportunities for new understandings so that students love those books even more. Remember that shout-from-the-rooftops kind of love?

Let's take the example of *Waiting Is Not Easy!*, one of the beloved installments in Mo Willems's Elephant and Piggie series. Since students are familiar with this book—or at least its characters—it will be easy to invite them in to a learning journey for deeper understanding. An easy place to start students on the path to deeper thinking is with the questions we pose and the discussion opportunities we provide while they are working with a particular text. For *Waiting Is Not Easy!* or any other student favorite, questions should move from literal and easy to recall to more thoughtful, requiring some consideration and connection from the minds of the little readers in front of you. Instead of simply asking how the characters are feeling in the story, your question could evolve into *What do the characters do or say that lets you know how they are feeling in different parts of the story?* The following table offers some examples of taking your questioning to the next level. When we change our questions, we change their thinking.

ASK THIS, NOT THAT!	
GENERAL UNDERSTANDING	DEEPER UNDERSTANDING
Who are the characters?	How can you tell how the characters are feeling?
What are Gerald and Piggie waiting for?	Why does Piggie's surprise for Gerald take so long?
What do big and bold words mean?	What do you notice about the types of print when the characters are talking? How does it help you as a reader?

Student interest sparks the motivation to engage in more rigorous reading and is a critical component of students' success with close reading practices in the early years of school. As teachers we are always searching for ways to make learning meaningful for our students; starting them off with texts they already know and love nudges them toward more advanced thinking without letting the joy of reading slip away. Beginning with books that students hold dear to their hearts provides a necessary scaffold before expecting students to think deeply about more complex texts. If we do not start close to home, it is unlikely we will be able to move very far away from home when we are reading, talking, and writing about texts with our students.

When students participate in new reading experiences with familiar texts, the new understandings they come away with are remarkable. You'll start to overhear them sharing their newfound knowledge with peers and adults alike. Some of their learning might even show up in their writing workshop pieces—a true sign that they've reached a higher level of learning with a text. We cannot let the joy of reading fade while we implement close reading strategies, for it is exactly that joy that keeps reading alive—and makes close reading possible—in our classrooms.

■ Choosing a Text

Identifying a text worthy of close reading is often one of the biggest hurdles to overcome when putting together a close reading plan. I have spent hours (literally) reading and searching with colleagues for texts that not only lend themselves to close, critical reading but are also connected to a particular unit of study or student interest. Choosing a text that lacks opportunities for multiple readings and new, meaningful understandings can often mean failure before we even begin reading. So how can we avoid this pitfall? How do we know if a book or article will work for close reading? Honestly, we really don't know for certain until we put it in front of our students. If only there were a foolproof system for selecting a text that we know for sure will work, right?

There are, however, some general guidelines to keep in mind to make choosing a worthy text a little easier, starting with knowing your books. In order to choose good books, we have to know good books. As teachers we must read widely and voraciously within the age range and interests of our students in order to have the best shot at success with our readers. Maria Walther taught me that this often means—because no teacher I know has extra time just waiting to be used up—getting creative with planning time, team meetings, or even the oh-so-important all-staff meetings. Just imagine how beneficial it would be for students if their teachers spent just fifteen minutes at a staff meeting reading, sharing, and discussing the latest and greatest in children's literature with one another. Administrators reading this, make it happen. Team leaders, craft your meeting agendas to include some time to read and talk about books; collaboration is imperative when choosing good texts for close reading. (See Figure 3.1.)

Figure 3.1
A fresh stack of books waits to be read by teachers during a PLC meeting.

It is important to point out that in the early elementary grades, a text suitable for close reading is most likely going to be a text that the students are not yet able to read independently. Chances are, the books students are independently reading—especially in the earliest years of school—don't lend themselves to the deep thinking and new learning we desire as an outcome of close reading. There is only so much you can do with a decodable book or sight-word reader, for instance. This is not to say that students cannot engage in deep thinking with their independent reading books; they certainly can. But their independent reading books will likely not support multiple readings for new purposes and understandings.

Our task when selecting a text is to remember that while students may not yet be able to read the book, article, or passage on their own, it must also not be so high-level that they cannot understand it or take away any new, transferable learning from it. When we wrap close reading into the shared experience of a read-aloud, we make an otherwise inaccessible text one that students come to know and understand very well. This is what makes the shared experience of the read-aloud so important for close reading with young readers, and it is a defining characteristic of how close reading in the primary grades differs from close reading in the intermediate and upper grades. Instead of asking students to read the text on their own, we support their thinking and understanding by reading it to them. As primary-grade teachers, it is our job to make texts for close reading accessible to our young readers.

Another defining characteristic of close reading is that it is carried out with a short piece of text. In the primary grades, since texts are typically already on the shorter side, it is possible to close-read with an entire text, but keep in mind that while you may initially read aloud a whole book or article with students, your closer look and subsequent readings might take place with only a small excerpt of that book or article. For example, after reading a whole picture book aloud to students, you might revisit just the pages that contain a literary device or a certain text structure you want students to notice and think more about and that would contribute to a "bigger picture" understanding of the text. You might read *The Day the Crayons Quit* (Daywalt 2013) in its entirety but then zoom in on just one of the crayon's letters for your close reading experience. There are several examples of taking a closer look at just one or a few pages of a book in the lessons outlined in the next chapter.

The Common Core State Standards place a strong emphasis on nonfiction or informational text; however, informational texts do not need to be the sole stars of the close reading experiences in your classroom. We sometimes default to nonfiction for close reading because it is "harder" or we think it contains more opportunities for students to learn. But plenty of fiction texts written for a young audience require students to do some careful noticing, to dig deeper, and to read and think critically. Especially now, with more complex fiction picture books hitting the shelves seemingly faster than ever, we are called to explore all the possibilities that fiction lays before us. Moreover, literary nonfiction is on the rise. These books that tell facts through story provide several meaningful learning opportunities to explore with close reading. Using what you know about your students as readers, consider texts—both fiction and nonfiction—that will align their interests with your instructional outcomes. The following table shows some of my favorite books for close reading.

SOME FAVORITE TEXTS FOR CLOSE READING WITH PRIMARY-GRADE READERS		
LITERARY	LITERARY NONFICTION	INFORMATIONAL
The Smallest Girl in the Smallest Grade by Justin Roberts, illus. Christian Robinson (2014)	*Giant Squid* by Candace Fleming, illus. Eric Rohmann (2016)	*Recess at 20 Below* by Cindy Lou Aillaud (2005)
The Day the Crayons Quit by Drew Daywalt, illus. Oliver Jeffers (2013)	*The Youngest Marcher: The Story of Audrey Faye Hendricks, a Young Civil Rights Activist* by Cynthia Levinson, illus. Vanessa Brantley Newton (2017)	*Pink Is for Blobfish: Discovering the World's Perfectly Pink Animals* by Jess Keating, illus. David DeGrand (2016)
Yard Sale by Eve Bunting, illus. Lauren Castillo (2015)	*One Plastic Bag: Isatou Ceesay and the Recycling Women of the Gambia* by Miranda Paul, illus. Elizabeth Zunon (2015)	*Fly Guy Presents: Weather* by Tedd Arnold (2016)
The Bad Seed by Jory John, illus. Pete Oswald (2017)		*Here We Are: Notes for Living on Planet Earth* by Oliver Jeffers (2017)
Blackout by John Rocco (2011)	*Ivan: The Remarkable True Story of the Shopping Mall Gorilla* by Katherine Applegate, illus. G. Brian Karas (2014)	*Spiders* by Nic Bishop (2007)
Triangle by Mac Barnett and Jon Klassen (2017)		*Desert Elephants* by Helen Cowcher (2011)
No, David! by David Shannon (1998)	*Give Bees a Chance* by Bethany Barton (2017)	*Bravo! Poems About Amazing Hispanics* by Margarita Engle, illus. Rafael López (2017)
The Night Gardener by Terry Fan and Eric Fan (2016)	*Ruth and the Green Book* by Calvin Alexander Ramsey and Gwen Strauss, illus. Floyd Cooper (2010)	*How to Swallow a Pig: Step-by-Step Advice from the Animal Kingdom* by Steve Jenkins and Robin Page (2015)
Don't Let the Pigeon Drive the Bus! by Mo Willems (2003)		
Jabari Jumps by Gaia Cornwall (2017)		

A final note about choosing a text for close reading involves passages we may find online that have been marketed and sold on web communities such as Teachers Pay Teachers. As teachers we must be careful and critical consumers of content created and tagged as "Close Reading Passages" because these texts often lack authenticity and opportunities for students to engage in higher-level thinking. Although I do not discount the tremendous amount of work that teachers put into creating these packets of passages, I caution their use and question their place in our classrooms. Predetermined passages that contain right-there evidence are not always the best option if we truly want our students to do some deep, real-world thinking. Rather, an authentic text chosen both for and because of the readers we have in front of us will give us the most bang for our buck. Texts that connect our young readers to their learning, to each other, and to the world around them—and that empower them to view themselves as readers and thinkers—are going to be most meaningful as they begin to shape their literacy lives.

■ Close Reading and Wordless Books

Wordless books and primary-grade close reading are a match made in literacy heaven. No words to read? No problem! Wordless books are perfect candidates for close reading experiences with early readers because the complexity of the stories within the illustrations invite young readers to notice, discuss, and ponder. They are especially successful as a launching point when you are just beginning close reading with your readers because the entire story emanates from the illustrations. Wordless books help instill the idea that illustrations are part of the text and that text evidence can come from illustrations.

WORDLESS BOOKS FOR CLOSE READING
Wave by Suzy Lee (2008)
Chalk by Bill Thomson (2010)
The Lion and the Mouse by Jerry Pinkney (2009)
Sidewalk Flowers by JonArno Lawson and Sydney Smith (2015)
The Girl and the Bicycle by Mark Pett (2014)
Spot, the Cat by Henry Cole (2016)
Unspoken by Henry Cole (2012)
Mirror by Jeannie Baker (2010)

■ Text Complexity

When we hear the words *rigor* and *complexity* our minds instantly think hard or difficult. Primary-grade teachers often struggle with the concept of rigorous content and question the idea of putting a "difficult" text in front of our young readers. The truth is, any text you put in front of a primary-grade reader could be complex to them, depending on their reading development and experiences with print. I used to think that if I put an overly hard, text-heavy book or passage in front of my students I was, by default, making them smarter. I thought, "Look what we're doing in kindergarten!" and proceeded to pat myself on the back. Those now cringe-worthy moments were where I started with close reading because I believed I had to; I thought that was what rigor and complexity meant. I now know, thankfully and with the help of some of my literacy heroes, that nothing comes from a forced struggle through a text that is way too difficult just for the sake of checking the "close reading" box. Doug Fisher and Nancy Frey remind us, "close reading doesn't mean that you simply distribute a complex reading and then exhort [students] to read it again and again until they understand it" (Fisher and Frey 2012, 8).

I have learned from Kylene Beers and Robert Probst (2015), two friends of literacy and close reading, that rigor cannot be achieved without relevance. In the primary grades, we create relevance by connecting reading experiences to our students' lives and setting a purpose that makes students want to read. Similarly, the term *complex* does not always have to mean difficult. I like to think of complexity with this guiding question in mind: Is this a text that will allow students to engage in deep thinking? Complexity and rigor are daunting terms, but when we put them in perspective, they are not so scary. Yes, text complexity is an important part of close reading, but it is not the only part. When we pair text complexity with students' interests and experiences, our close reading practice becomes most beneficial.

Choosing a text worthy of close reading is no easy task, so let's start the conversation by thinking about our students as independent readers, or simply readers if they are not yet decoding words on the page. What kinds of things are they coming across in the books they read that could support a close reading experience? What texts—print or digital—will help students move toward attainment of close reading skills or strategies? These guiding questions assist us as we search for the perfect text to closely read with our students.

Those same questions led the way for me as I prepared for close reading with a first-grade class. After chatting with the teacher and conferring with some of the children during reading, I realized that many were missing the central message of the books they were reading. Their independent reading books begged them to deduce a central message, but they just omitted this aspect of reading. Most of them could recall and describe the characters, setting, problem, and solution but struggled with what the book was saying. Because many of their books had central messages worthy of study, that became the focus for our close reading experience.

I catalog all my "teaching" books using an online database (If you already do this, then you know it is life-changing. If you do not already do this, do it. Now. Call me. I'll help you.), so a quick search of "central message" in my database brought up all the books I already had in my library that I could use for this close reading experience. A simple Google search will also provide you with great books for exploring a central message.

Yard Sale by Eve Bunting (2015) provided the context I was looking for—a strong central message blanketed in a beautiful story with which the students in this class could connect. It is also a story that begs to be read more than once and for different purposes (jackpot!). After several reading experiences with this book, students took character clues from the young girl in the story to develop their thinking about the central message. Together, we examined the girl's thoughts and actions throughout the story, recorded those thoughts and actions on chart paper, and slowly developed the book's central message. A guiding question for my readers was: Based on the girl's thoughts and actions, what does the author want us to know after reading this book? This question is a complex one for primary-grade students, but using close reading to build up to that complexity layer by layer equipped these little readers to tackle that complexity successfully.

After using close reading to deeply explore the central message of *Yard Sale*, the students were more capable of thinking about and articulating the messages they encountered in other books during independent reading, such as *You Are (Not) Small* by Anna Kang (2014) or *Ballet Cat: The Totally Secret Secret* by Bob Shea (2015)—two easily lovable books with important messages that these first graders could now decipher independently.

Grasping the central message of the books the students were inde-pendently reading was an aspect of their comprehension that had needed a little boost. In seizing this opportunity for a close reading experience, I was able to use multiple readings of *Yard Sale* as a scaffold for students to develop an understanding of the book's central message and to become more able to identify the central message when reading on their own. By keeping our readers at the forefront of our thinking about close reading, we can choose texts that students will happily revisit several times and that model transferable skills and strategies they will need as they develop their capacity for independent reading

◼ Multiple Readings

Repeated readings are another nonnegotiable aspect of close reading, and planning effective close reading lessons involves laying a solid foundation of understanding through an initial reading of the text, and then layering subsequent readings of that same text for the purpose of deepening students' comprehension. When selecting a text, we must keep in mind that the content of the text—words, illustrations, photographs, and so on—must be rich enough and relevant enough to sustain learning and thinking throughout several reading experiences.

In the pages that follow, I use the terms first reading, second reading, and third reading for ease of understanding the close reading progression, but I want to point out that close reading will not always follow such a rigid structure. There will be times when your first and second readings look very similar to one another, or when you need more than three readings to accomplish the learning objectives. The point here is that you do not need to finish the first reading and its corresponding activities then move directly into the second reading and its set of possible activities. Give yourself permission to let these multiple readings flow naturally as you meet your students where they are with what they need.

Each reading of a text should offer something new that supports students' understanding. It helps to start broadly with the first reading of a text so that the following readings can be narrowed in focus yet heightened in comprehension and critical thinking. When close reading is done well, students should understand more and more with each reading of the text. Using Fisher and Frey's (2014b) guiding questions for close reading as a framework, we can explore the progression of a close reading experience in the primary grades.

◼ What Does the Text Say?

The first reading of a text is often the most important because it will set the stage for the learning and thinking that will follow. This initial reading is sometimes called a "cold read" and is carried out with little frontloading so that the students are the ones constructing their own thinking. During this first reading for enjoyment and basic understanding, we use the guiding question, What does the text say? To really get to the core of the question, we know that our first instructional move must be to guide students toward a general, surface-level understanding of the text. Before students can dig deeper and uncover new meaning, they must first be able to recall, restate, or retell the key ideas or events in a text.

Using the standards as our instructional anchor, the first reading of a text should focus on things like summarizing and retelling, story elements, or main idea and details. While this initial reading is not limited to just these aspects of reading comprehension, these particular skills cast a wide enough net that we can then pull in as we focus on more specific thinking within the text. Students will rely on their general understanding of a text as they begin to analyze different components of a text across multiple readings.

One of my favorite methods to use with students during the first reading of a literary text is the *Somebody Wanted But So* (SWBS) (Macon, Bewell, and Vogt 1991) strategy for summarizing. It is great when you want students to generate an initial understanding because it affords students an opportunity to perfect their summarizing skills as they internalize a text that will be revisited in the coming days. Take this example from the picture book *The Smallest Girl in the Smallest Grade* by Justin Roberts (2014). After our initial read-aloud experience, students participated in a whole-class collaborative conversation as we pieced together our SWBS summary (see Figure 3.2). You'll notice I am asking general understanding questions to move the conversation along as we create our book summary.

> **Teacher:** *Who would you say is our most important character in this story?*
>
> **Student 1:** *I think it is the girl.*
>
> **Student 2:** *I agree with [S1] because she helped the school.*
>
> **T:** *Can anyone remember that character's name? Who is our somebody?*
>
> **All:** *Sally!*
>
> **T:** *Yes, that is her name! What did we learn about Sally early on in the story?*
>
> **Student 3:** *We learned that she is the smallest.*
>
> **S1:** *And we learned that she is always noticing things.*
>
> **T:** *Talk with your learning partner about the things Sally was noticing.*

(Students discuss and share.)

T: *If these are things she was noticing, as we continue our summary, what could we say that she wanted?*

Student 4: *Sally wanted to make her school nicer.*

S2: *And she also wanted to make her friends be nice.*

T: *Okay. So if we are writing our summary together, what would we say? Turn and talk to your learning partner about how our summary might look and sound.*

(Students discuss and give a thumbs-up when ready to share.)

Figure 3.2

This completed chart shows a class-generated summary following an initial reading of a text.

The rest of the SWBS activity carries on in a similar fashion until students are able to collectively craft a summary they are pleased with. My role as the facilitator is to ask general understanding questions about characters and key ideas in order to fuel student thinking while folding in opportunities for student talk.

During a first reading of an informational text, the instructional focus becomes a general understanding of the main topic and key details. A simple way to capture this learning is to collectively create a concept map on chart paper to show the class's thinking. This tried-and-true instructional strategy records thinking so that students can refer to it during future reading experiences as they work with the text in other ways.

Another approach for the first reading of a text is to ask each student (or pair of students) to recall a fact they learned or that resonated with them during the reading. They can either write this fact down or share it orally while the teacher serves as the scribe. Students can then work together to figure out what all of those shared facts have in common, which helps them to discover the main topic or main purpose of the text on their own. Figure 3.3 shows the thinking of some kindergarten students after an initial reading

Figure 3.3
Students used sticky notes to record new facts they learned from *Recess at 20 Below*.

of the informational book *Recess at 20 Below* by Cindy Lou Aillaud (2005), an anchor text in their unit of study on winter.

Whatever lesson ideas or teaching and learning strategies you choose to pair with the first reading of a text, always remember that your initial goal is for students to exhibit a general understanding of the plot or the information being presented. It is on this foundation of understanding that students will build their way up to new ideas and new ways of thinking about texts. The strategies shared here are just a few of many that will send students on their way to deeper comprehension.

■ Questioning and Discussion During a First-Reading Experience

Text-dependent questioning (or TDQ), like rigor and complexity, is fancy terminology that came right along with the onset of close reading expectations. It is also a term, like rigor and complexity, that was not so scary before we had a name for it. Remember when we just called them questions? In fact, TDQ has become one of the most feared acronyms in a profession that loves making acronyms for everything. Think about it. We go to RtI meetings after PLC meetings because an LL student's WCPM on the F&P is impacting their mastery of the CCSS in ELA. Acronyms galore! I remember the first time my evaluator emailed me and said she'd like to observe a reading lesson with TDQs. Full disclosure: I had to google what it meant. Some people say TGIF; I say TGFG: Thank God for Google.

Doug Fisher, Nancy Frey, and their colleagues who collaborated on the book *Text-Dependent Questions: Pathways to Close and Critical Reading* (2014) provide teachers with a framework for the kinds of questions to ask as you move through close reading experiences with students. With *The Smallest Girl in the Smallest Grade*, the questions posed to the students were all basic comprehension questions that would assist them as they constructed their short summary of the text. Similarly, when working with *Recess at 20 Below*, questions focused on a general retelling of facts learned in order to craft the students' idea of the main topic. The following table lists examples of text-dependent questions for both fiction and informational texts.

TEXT-DEPENDENT QUESTIONS FOR GENERAL UNDERSTANDING	
FICTION	INFORMATIONAL
Who is the main character?	
What is the problem in the story?	What is the main topic?
What events in the story make up the beginning, middle, and end?	What are some facts you learned?
Where does the story take place?	What facts did you already know? How did you learn them?
What is this story about?	

■ Student Ownership During a First Reading

Student-led learning environments are becoming increasingly important as we teach our students to be twenty-first-century thinkers and leaders. Throughout close reading experiences, we must not forget to look for those little pockets of opportunity during which our students can take on some of the teaching and leadership roles. The following ideas are meant to promote student ownership during the first reading of a text.

■ Students as Record Keepers

In Chapter 2, I shared how we can allow our students to keep track of their thinking through the use of a thinking trail. After some teacher-modeled experiences with this kind of sketch note-taking, students are able to own the process and the activity. With primary-grade students I find it still helpful for the teacher to plan the "think points" at which to pause, sketch, and write, but students can now begin to keep their own record of the text instead of joining a teacher-led whole-class thinking trail. See Figure 3.4 for a second grader's thinking trail for the book *Mufaro's Beautiful Daughters* by John Steptoe (2008).

To further student ownership, one student can lead the thinking trail, positioning herself near the chart paper and tracking her thinking for the rest of the class to see. This not only supports a student-led learning environment but also provides a mentor text for students who are completing thinking trails of their own. Inviting students to lead the thinking trail is an instructional tactic that works well with most students, especially with students who get squirrelly or off-task easily, because they have a responsibility to capture their important thinking for the class (but I'm sure none of you ever have squirrelly or off-task students).

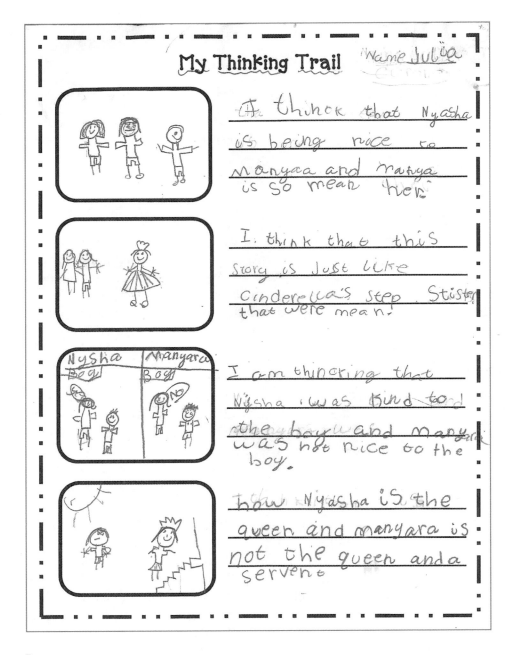

Figure 3.4
Pause for "think points" so students can jot their thinking during the read-aloud.

■ Students as Discussion Leaders

As students become more confident in discussing initial understanding questions, the responsibility for the questioning can be released to them. Rather than viewing me as the keeper of the questions, students take ownership by asking their own questions. This, again, comes after students have had a lot of exposure to the types of text-dependent questions expected during a first reading of a text. Once they have learned from your modeling how to ask questions about characters, tricky words, and key events or facts, they are ready to ask their own questions. Students write their questions (or dictate them for you to write) on note cards or sticky notes and jump at the chance to ask their questions when their card or sticky note is drawn. My young readers beam with pride as they lead the class in a discussion of their questions. As an added component of ownership, give the student-questioner the autonomy to choose whether she'd like her peers to participate in a turn-and-talk partner conversation or a whole-class collaborative conversation. As you know, any opportunity the students have to "be the teacher" is extremely engaging and motivating, especially for students who think they already are the teacher (but I'm sure none of you have those students either). You will not have time for each student to ask his or her question during the first reading session, but it is nice to save the questions to launch a review or refresher discussion before beginning each subsequent reading.

■ Annotation During a First Reading

Chapter 2 talks about some different kinds of annotation that work well with young readers and writers engaged in close reading. The first reading of a text offers an opportunity to engage in annotation work that tracks student thinking during or after the first reading of a text. A thinking trail or sharing thinking related to the text are both acceptable annotations during this initial reading. These kinds of annotation make student thinking immediately visible, showing you the range of understanding that students are starting with.

Another form of annotation that is perfect for an initial reading of a text are search and find annotations. You will recall from Chapter 2 that with this kind of annotation, students are marking up a text as they read and locate letters, words, types of sentences, or other print concepts you may be studying at the time. This annotation requires young readers to look closely at the words on the page and boosts their confidence as they begin to see themselves as real readers. For example, during our first reading of *Recess at 20 Below*, even though students could not yet read the words independently, they could recognize the consonant blends we had been practicing in order to figure out some beginning sounds. After reading together, we took just a few minutes to locate and mark words that contained consonant blends beginning with the letter *s*. Marking these words provided students with a real context for the consonant blend work they were already doing in the classroom (see Figure 3.5).

Keep in mind that annotating will not be your sole instructional purpose during the first reading of a text. There will still be some initial comprehension work that needs to take place as well. Annotation is a skill that you fold in carefully and purposefully as an ingredient of deeper text understanding or of primary-grade reading skills.

■ How Does the Text Work?

During a rereading of the text, the question How does the text work? serves as the anchor for the learning that will take place. Together with your readers, you begin to look at the structure of a text. Things like how the text is organized, the perspective from which it is written, the word choices or craft moves made by the author, the artistic choices made by the illus-

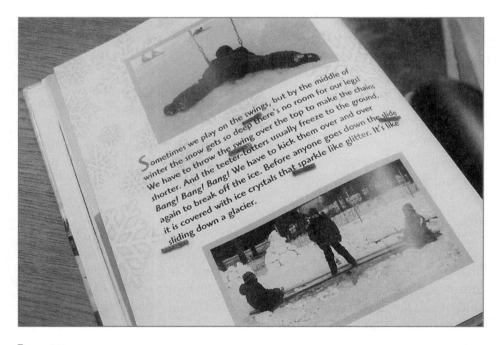

Figure 3.5
Students use search and find annotations to locate and read words with *s* blends.

trator, and the development of the plot or main idea all become important when thinking about how a text works. Learning opportunities that tackle how the functionality of a text impacts readers and how the choices made by an author or illustrator are vital to creating meaning are central to taking student understanding to the next level after their initial understanding of a text.

A good place to start is with the features of the text that make it complex, or worthy of close reading, in the first place. What was it about this text that made it a good candidate to closely read with your students? Once these aspects are determined, it is easier to decide on a focus for your second reading of the text. And remember, the good news is we do not expect our students to arrive at or discover this kind of learning on their own. Once again, we wrap things like text structure, vocabulary, and plot or information development in the blanket of a read-aloud experience, inviting students to experience and understand how the text works right along with us.

Another important go-to question to keep at the forefront of our thinking as we guide students to understand how a text works is What do you notice? Challenging students to notice as much as possible about how a text is put together will strengthen their understanding of the text as a whole. When students notice a lot, their comprehension and their thinking improves a lot. Inviting student noticing is a great way to hook them into deep conversations about the inner workings of a text.

■ Vocabulary

New vocabulary is a common source of text complexity in the texts I choose to use when engaging in close reading with my students. It is also often a barrier to students' understanding of how a text works. If your experience with Common Core English Language Arts Standard 4—Ask and answer questions about unknown words in a text (National Governors Association Center for Best Practices and Council of Chief State School Officers 2010) is similar to mine, then it is probably a standard that you'll "get to later" because there are more important things to do. If your experience is really like mine, then you have also thought about how hard it is for young readers to determine the difference between words for which they know the meaning and words for which they do not know the meaning. I may have even said, "They don't even know that they don't even know what those words mean!" I mean, can't we just focus on getting students to read words they know rather than asking them to pick out words they don't know? Sigh. Alas, just as we arm our students with strategies to decode unknown words, we must also—from the early years of school—teach them what new words mean while simultaneously teaching them strategies to decipher the tricky vocabulary they may come across as readers.

In my classroom, when looking at word choice or vocabulary presented in the text, my students call themselves word detectives. I like this term not only because it keeps with my theme of close reading being a way to read like a detective (What primary teacher doesn't love a good theme?) but because it also signals to students that they will be doing some figure-it-out kind of work with words as we read together. When my students are word detectives, they know that they will be learning new words and working with their peers to deduce word meanings. Figure 3.6 shows a proud word detective after tackling some new vocabulary learning.

Figure 3.6
A proud close reader shows off her word detective journal.

A helpful teaching and learning strategy for young word detectives is an adaptation of Patricia Cunningham's (2009) Three Read-Aloud Words strategy. This strategy not only provides an opportunity for students to examine the words an author has chosen but also allows them to expand their vocabulary while searching for word-meaning clues within the text.

Students will closely listen for three (or two, or one, or four, depending on your lesson goals) words that you have preselected as essential for understanding the current text and that are also words that students may come across or use in their future endeavors as readers and writers. As you read aloud and come across the words you have selected, students are invited to indicate they have heard the word by yelling, "STOP!" followed by the word. From there a discussion ensues regarding the word, the context or sentence in which it appears, and, eventually, the word's meaning.

Taking Cunningham's strategy a step further into close reading requires students to think about how they were able to figure out the word's meaning and provide evidence for their determined meaning. Were there any clues in the words or illustrations that hinted at the meaning? Are there any real-world contexts in which we hear or see these words? These questions allow our young readers to practice providing evidence or rationale to support their thinking in the context of a group reading experience.

When I am working with students who are closely reading for new vocabulary understandings using this strategy, I like to keep a record of their thinking about new words. I usually keep this record in a table format, calling it our "I Am a Word Detective" table. (The super-original-name-creator strikes again!) In this table, I record the word for which students are listening along with their ideas for what they think the word means. I honor and record all thinking, regardless of its proximity to the word's actual meaning, (1) so that students know their thinking is important to our learning and (2) because this initial thinking provides a variety of baseline understandings that can be refined, reconstructed, or redirected after digging a little deeper into the text. From there, our discussion moves into what each word actually means, and how students were able to figure it out using evidence, prior knowledge, or intertextual connections.

The "I Am a Word Detective" table is something that can be completed in front of students using the board, chart paper, or a document camera. I sometimes have students (mostly second graders) complete the table using their clipboards along with me, but definitely not always and definitely not when their completing the chart hinders their ability to participate in the vocabulary learning. A student "I Am a Word Detective" table is included in Appendix D. Regardless of how you choose to bring it to life, this table holds students' thinking as they move from general wonderings about a word to really digging in and determining the word's meaning.

Figure 3.7 shows a completed "I Am a Word Detective" table using the text *The Smallest Girl in the Smallest Grade* (see Figure 3.7). Students were listening for the words *abandoned, continue,* and *transform.* After coming across each word, students worked together to brainstorm what they thought the word meant before we looked closely in the text to examine the word's context and its connection to the illustration on the page in which it appeared. Students shared their evidence-based thinking as well as any connections students make to the text that allowed us to arrive at the word meanings together as a class.

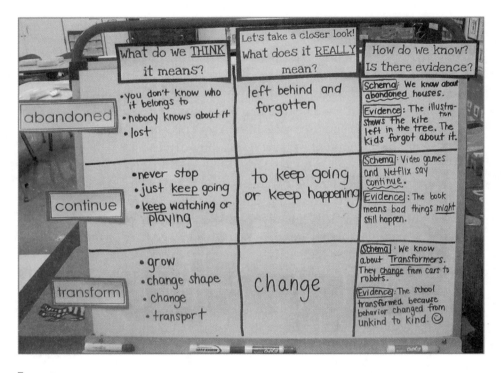

Figure 3.7
Student vocabulary learning is captured using an "I Am a Word Detective" table like this one.

Another example (see Figure 3.8) comes from a close reading experience with the text *One Plastic Bag: Isatou Ceesay and the Recycling Women of the Gambia* by Miranda Paul (2015). Students here were using just a two-page excerpt from the text to notice unfamiliar words and annotate by circling them. As a class, we made a list of students' unfamiliar vocabulary words with the intent of further exploring the two that occurred most frequently as unknown to students. We ended up taking a closer look at *swarm* and *forage* by examining the surrounding text for evidence of the words' meanings and discussing why each word was important to the overall story. Finally, we brainstormed instances where these words might appear in their own writing. I like this activity because it allows students to practice picking out what they don't know and provides them with a safe space to share their "unknowns" with classmates. Unknown words are celebrated as a chance for students to learn more about a text.

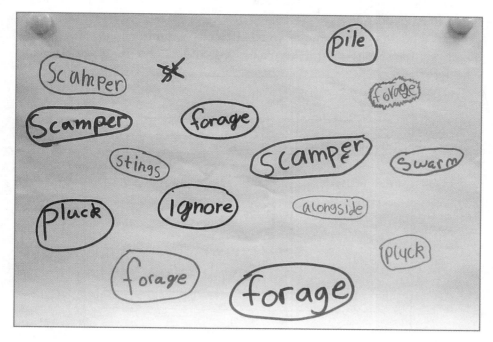

Figure 3.8
Students record unfamiliar words during a close reading experience in second grade.

No matter how you choose to support students as they discover new word meanings, I recommend allowing them to keep track of their vocabulary learning in some way. My students keep word detective journals that house one word from each of our close reading experiences. If we have discovered the meanings to a few words in one close reading experience (like we did with *The Smallest Girl in the Smallest Grade* and *One Plastic Bag*), students get to choose which word they would like to include in their journals. On each page of the journal, students first record which book it was that we read together. I like to use a thumbnail photo of the front cover of the text because, let's be honest, sometimes it takes more time for students the write the title of the book than there are hours in the school day. They then write the vocabulary word of their choosing, its newly uncovered meaning, and an illustration of the word as it relates to the text. Students will need plenty of modeled guidance and support as they complete their word detective journals, but they will move toward more independence after some extended practice. Figure 3.9 shows my teacher-modeled example of a word detective journal, and Figure 3.10 depicts an example from a second-grade student. A template for the journal can be found in Appendix E.

My students keep their word detective journals in their book boxes so they can be quickly accessed and added to when students

Figure 3.9
A teacher-modeled example of a page from the word detective journal.

discover new word meanings during guided or independent reading. Not to mention they love to read these journals over and over again whenever possible. They are so proud of their detective work! Your word detectives will fill their journals with new words throughout the year, both within and outside close reading experiences, and they will leave your classroom with a bank of vocabulary words to take with them as they progress through school.

There are several vocabulary strategies that work well as part of a close reading sequence. Use the strategies that are tried-and-true and that work

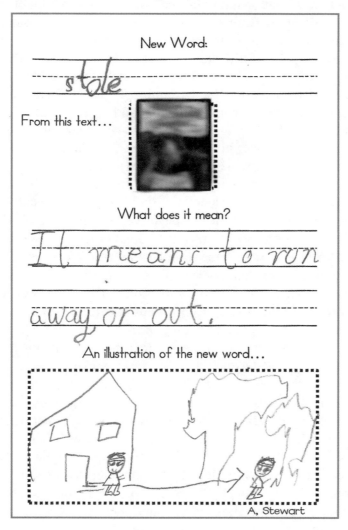

Figure 3.10
This word detective journal page shows a second grader's vocabulary learning.

for your students. Trust yourself and lean on best practices for word learning to have the greatest impact on your students.

■ Text Structure

In the same way that vocabulary is important to how a text works, so too is text structure. How a text is put together and organized impacts student comprehension (for better or worse). It is important for young readers to notice and have experience with examining text structures and thinking about authors' organizational moves because they will no doubt encounter more and more complex features as time goes on. While our primary-grade readers certainly do not need to know every text feature or every way to organize a text, it is helpful if they at least understand that different texts have different structures and that authors make choices about the way their text is presented to readers. When examining text structure, we look at things like how an author organizes the text and the text features—such as format, headings, author's notes, and graphics—that are included to facilitate understanding or cluster information in certain places.

Informational texts provide a great context for taking a closer look at structure. My students absolutely adore the informational books by Jess Keating and David DeGrand, especially *Pink Is for Blobfish* and especially when we get to the naked mole rat page (Naked! Eeep!). These vibrant books are chock-full of photographs, little-known facts, different types of print, and colorful graphics. And while Keating and DeGrand's books are often at the top of my student book-request list, they pose significant challenges to inexperienced readers of nonfiction. I mentioned earlier in this chapter that infusing close reading practices with texts students love will maximize both engagement and learning. *Pink Is for Blobfish* put me in the perfect position to do just that—to take a text that students love and move them toward a deeper understanding of it (again, jackpot!).

This close reading experience with *Blobfish* came about spontaneously (I love when that happens!) after I had read some of the book aloud during a morning meeting with first graders who were in the midst of an animal unit. These students were instantly hooked on this weird, funny book. I began to notice, however, that despite their high engagement with this text, their accuracy levels were low, and comprehension even lower, when they were reading independently. One clear barrier to their comprehension was the layout of the text, illustrations, and photographs on each double-page spread. Students were not yet able to make sense of how to go about reading a text like this (Where do I start? Do I read all of it? When do I read this part?), and they lacked understanding of how the different text features worked together to provide a complete profile of each weird, pink animal.

I wanted students to be able to understand the book as much as they loved it, but I also wanted to be sure I did not kill the joy of reading by bringing it into a close reading experience without specific goals in mind. I have had many failed attempts at close reading by taking an enjoyable book and beating all the joy out of it for the sake of covering the standards. I gathered the students together and we began a second reading, with me guiding them. I knew I had to start small in order to convey the big understanding about text features and structure that I was envisioning. We began by zooming in on just two animals, hippopotamuses and (of course) naked mole rats. Together, we noticed words and text features like types of print, photographs, and illustrations, drawing parallels between the two pages in order to discuss similarities. We then discussed the purpose and content of each text feature that the students noticed (see Figure 3.11). I kept track of student thinking as they determined how to make sense of the structure of this particular text. Using close reading strategies to notice and name informational text features gave the learning a context and was much more meaningful and engaging to them than teaching the text features in isolation.

I cannot stress enough the importance of providing opportunities for students to transfer and apply the learning from a close reading experience to their independent reading lives. After reading and discussing *Pink Is for Blobfish*, students got busy with the informational books in their book boxes, searching for text features or structures that were similar to or different from the ones we had just examined together. One student noticed that his *Fly Guy Presents: Weather* book had hand-drawn illustrations combined with real photographs, just like *Blobfish* did. Another student noticed quick facts in her National Geographic Kids book about frogs that were similar to those presented in *Blobfish*, but that were displayed for the reader using a different text structure than the one Keating and DeGrand chose. This close reading experience provided—as any close reading experience should—an opportunity for students to deeply and collaboratively engage in a complex text with the intent to learn and to use that learning to better understand other books they choose to keep stocked in their book bins for independent reading.

■ Text-Illustration Connection

Another important aspect of how a text works is the connection between the words on the page and the illustrations or photographs that accompany

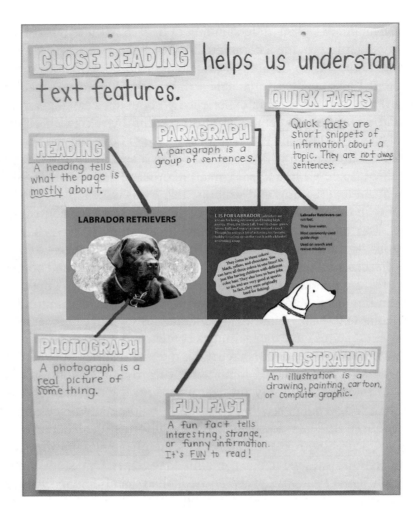

Figure 3.11
Use close reading to help students better understand the features of informational text.

them. Standard 7 of the Common Core State Standards (CCSS) for reading challenges us to get students thinking about how the text and illustrations or photographs work together to offer another layer of understanding or discovery that either might not be able to do if they stood alone. I call this the forgotten standard because, while we often superficially discuss with students the content of the illustrations or photographs, we tend to stay on the surface instead of pushing students (and ourselves) to think about how the pictures enhance our understanding or make us think about the text in a new way.

Pictures are critical to the development of early readers, and sometimes the only part of a text that students are able to "read." Our youngest readers use pictures to gather clues that help them decode words and comprehend what they are reading. Pictures support them as readers and give them confidence as they work to make sense of the words on the page. Illustrations and photographs play an important role for these readers in developing a deep understanding of a text.

A picture-perfect text for engaging the connection between text and illustration is *Giant Squid* by Candace Fleming and illustrated by Eric Rohmann. After some initial work with this book, the group of second graders mentioned earlier noticed that on each page, only one part of the giant squid is pictured. Whether it was the eye, the tentacles, or the mantle, students noticed that they never got a full picture of the giant squid until the very end of the book. This was a very important noticing that led to a discussion about how the text works and why those illustrations are important to understanding not only the words on the page but the book as a whole. Here is a snapshot of that discussion:

> **Student 1:** *I notice that you only see part of the giant squid on every page.*
>
> **Student 2:** *Yeah. Except at the end you see the whole thing.*
>
> **Teacher:** *That's such an interesting noticing! Why do you think that is?*
>
> **S1:** *Because it has to match the words.*
>
> **Student 3:** *And because the author doesn't want you to know what it looks like until the end.*
>
> **S1:** *Yeah, so you keep reading until the end because sometimes you want to stop reading, but if they put the picture at the end, you keep on reading.*
>
> **T:** *I love your* thinking *here. What about these two words from the story:* mystery *and* lurk? *Do those words give you any ideas about the way these illustrations are set up?*
>
> **S3:** *Oh yeah! Because it's a mystery you can't see the whole thing at one time.*

S1: And scientists don't find it very much and maybe if they do, it is only little parts they see.

S2: It takes them a long time to see the whole squid so you have to wait 'til the end like the scientists have to wait forever for it.

This kind of thinking comes from deep engagement with and a lot of exposure to the text. Close reading makes these conversations possible for the young readers in our classrooms. Building on this student-generated discussion, students were asked to write some of their thoughts about illustrations playing a big role in how the text *Giant Squid* works. Figure 3.12 shows a student's thinking about the choices that the author and illustrator made and how it contributed to her understanding of new vocabulary.

It might be hard to envision your students noticing and talking about such specific aspects of a text, but when you've introduced, modeled, and practiced noticing across several learning experiences, it becomes the norm. This kind of deep thinking and discussion can emerge because you have set the stage and made it possible. Encourage, believe in, and follow your students' thinking as they become the skilled readers you have taught them to be.

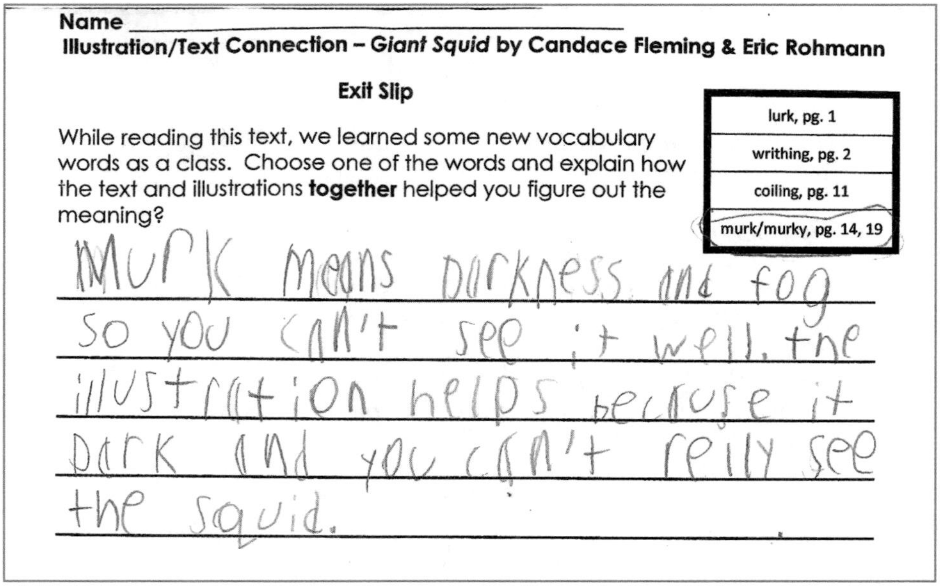

Name _____

Illustration/Text Connection – *Giant Squid* by Candace Fleming & Eric Rohmann

Exit Slip

While reading this text, we learned some new vocabulary words as a class. Choose one of the words and explain how the text and illustrations **together** helped you figure out the meaning?

| lurk, pg. 1 |
| writhing, pg. 2 |
| coiling, pg. 11 |
| murk/murky, pg. 14, 19 |

Murk means darkness and fog so you can't see it well. the illustration helps because it dark and you can't reily see the squid.

Figure 3.12

A student responds in writing to a text-dependent question that requires her to think carefully about the illustrations in *Giant Squid*.

■ Questioning and Discussion During a Second Reading Experience

The questions we pose to our students about how a text works require them to think about things like text structure, vocabulary, and how the choices made by authors and illustrators impact how a text is read and understood. These questioning and discussion opportunities are folded into the learning that is taking place within the close reading lesson. You do not need a separate "question time" after reading. Rather, students can discuss their thinking in response to questions about how the text works at any point throughout the lesson. Think of it as a sprinkling here and there of pauses for rich discussion.

With young readers and writers, it is often we teachers who ask the questions, but keep in mind that when modeled and practiced enough, we can gradually release the questioning responsibility to the students. The following table contains tried-and-true text-dependent questions that have to do with how a text works.

| TEXT-DEPENDENT QUESTIONS FOR HOW THE TEXT WORKS ||
FICTION	INFORMATIONAL
What does this word mean? Have you heard it before? Are there any clues in the text to help us figure it out? How does this character change from the beginning of the story to the end of the story? What events brought about the change? What moves did the author or illustrator make to help you better understand the story? How does what you see in the illustrations help you better understand the text?	What does this word mean? Have you heard it before? Are there any clues in the text to help us figure it out? What text features do you notice in this book? How do those help you as reader? How does what you see in the photographs or pictures help you better understand the text?

■ Annotation During a Second Reading Experience

Elements of annotation that might be used during a second reading include noting important vocabulary, searching for and finding different text features, or examining and marking purposeful language. Students might also expand their initial thinking annotations from the first reading. Revisiting their thinking trails or adding to their Share Your Thinking documents again provides a visible account of students' evolution of understanding. Remember to give annotation a purpose, letting students know why they are annotating and what they can do with their annotations when they revisit a text.

After an initial reading of *The Snowy Day* (Keats 1962), my students and I looked at some of the vocabulary words Keats used in the story and determined their meaning together. Students used their own copies of the text to annotate by drawing a picture clue on a small sticky note and placing it next to the unfamiliar word. This way, when they returned to the text for subsequent readings, they had a clue to remind them what the word was and what it meant. Similarly, in *The Smallest Girl in the Smallest Grade*, we used whole-class annotation by underlining the powerful language that Justin Roberts uses throughout the story and discussing how those words affected us as readers (see Figure 3.13).

Figure 3.13
Digital annotations show student thinking about the words and phrases an author uses.

■ What Does the Text Mean: Third Reading and Beyond

Meaning and new ideas become the focus of later readings of a text during a close reading sequence. The question *What does the text mean?* implies so much more than just asking students to figure out a predetermined meaning we've decided for them. After spending several days with a text, our readers are able to think beyond our parameters toward new, bigger thinking that moves them forward as readers. During this stage of close reading, we invite students into learning opportunities that help them better understand the text from a "big picture" view. Text evidence and student schema become increasingly important as young readers continue to explore and go deeper with things like character development, central message, author's purpose, and their own opinions.

Meaning making is unique to each reader. A book, article, or other piece of text can mean something different to each and every reader who encounters it because the variety of readers who grace our classrooms all have different experiences that shape their meaning creation (Rosenblatt 1978). It is our charge as primary-grade teachers to teach students what meaning is by arming them with strategies that help them understand their own meaning-making processes.

It is during a third or fourth reading of the text that you might choose to fold in another text or piece of text, encouraging connections between the two while also sharpening students' comparing and contrasting skills. While you do not want to lose the deep reading of the initial text, bringing another text into the mix can often assist with student meaning making and discovery of new ideas related to the topic or subject being read. If you believe that student understanding of the initial text for which you are using close reading will be enhanced by bringing another text into the experience, I say go for it.

■ Determining Importance

A key step toward meaning making is determining the importance of words, sentences, events, facts, or characters that have helped shape student thinking throughout different readings of a text and that will contribute to their overall understanding. This can be a challenging task for young readers who do not quite understand the difference between important and unimportant items. Jack just ran out of the classroom: Important. Heidi has too many pencils in her toolbox: Less important. Sometimes it seems as though our days are a constant loop of reminding students that some things are important, while other things are very, very far from important. Nevertheless, teaching students how to determine the importance of little pieces of the text will assist them in reaching new understandings of the text as a whole.

Every time we think aloud while modeling how we determine whether something is important, we are teaching students how to do it themselves. We show students how to pick out a sentence, illustration, paragraph, or any other aspect of the text, and we tell them why we believe it to be important. Standing on our shoulders, students learn to think critically before deeming a piece of the text to be important in the big-picture view of the text. It is critical in this stage of the reading to honor the pieces of the text that students deem important, keeping in mind that what is important to one student might not necessarily be so to another student. Throughout this phase of reading, students learn to share, discuss, and defend their important parts, and to discern what is and is not vital to understanding the text as a whole. Students can then take all the smaller, important pieces of a text and put them together to determine the central message, main idea, or big understanding.

During our third reading experience with *Ruth and the Green Book* (Ramsey and Strauss 2010), students worked collaboratively to determine some important words and sentences from each page. This was a perfect opportunity for students to use Wikki Stix for annotation. We then took those important pieces and analyzed them together as a class as we crafted our interpretation of the book's message. By starting small and getting bigger, students were able to move their comprehension from basic recall and retell to an understanding of the message built in to the story.

■ Synthesizing

Synthesizing is a pivotal strategy for close reading and goes hand in hand with determining importance and tracking changes in thinking that occur while reading a text. In order to create meaning or arrive at new thinking, students must be able to synthesize what they have read. Just as we nudge our young readers to determine importance, we must also teach them to combine their existing schema with all the learning from each reading of the text in order to draw their own conclusions and think about the text in a new way.

Synthesizing comes into play when students are looking closely at a character in the text. Let's think for a minute about Pigeon from *Don't Let the Pigeon Drive the Bus!* (Willems 2003). Pigeon's words and actions provide the perfect context for students to synthesize their characteristics of him after several readings of the story. At first, they might think one thing about Pigeon, but as they read on and read again, their thoughts about him may change. If students are to determine the characteristics of Pigeon, they must think about Pigeon's words and actions, their own schema about how people (birds) act, and the features of the text that relate to Pigeon. Synthesizing all this learning that has occurred across multiple readings of the book allows young readers to form a bigger understanding of Pigeon. It also provides them with a new lens through which they can look at other favorite characters. Figure 3.14 shows the synthesizing work of some kindergarten students.

As students learn to synthesize, they begin to keep track of their thinking. They begin to pay attention to themselves as readers. Close reading experiences allow our students to think about their journey with a text and consider how that journey has changed their understanding—where their thinking was and where their thinking is now.

Figure 3.14
Kindergarten students share their thinking about Pigeon after multiple readings.

■ Author's Purpose

As we learn more about close reading, it seems that true close reading cannot be separated from a close look at the role of the author or illustrator. On the surface, young readers know that authors write the words and illustrators draw the pictures. But if we challenge our students to deeply engage with a text, we must also challenge them to think about authors and illustrators as real people who write for the same reasons that we encourage our students to write. With close reading we want our students to move beyond basic purposes for writing, such as persuade, inform, and entertain. We want them to be able to look through the lens of the author as they think about why a text was written. Think of it as asking your young readers to assume the role of the author or illustrator. If this were your book, why would you want kids to read it, or what would you want them to learn from it? Sometimes the author's note or bio at the end of the book gives a clue as to why a book was written. Students love that little peek into an author's motivation, not to mention that author's notes themselves make for amazing close reading opportunities. Even without an author's note, though, students are able to make informed speculations about an author or illustrator's purpose because they have spent so much time reading and analyzing the text in different ways.

■ Forming Opinions

Once students are armed with learning from several experiences with the same text, they are ready to form their own opinions about topics or ideas that have arisen from those readings. Forming an opinion and supporting it with evidence from the text is one of the last pieces of close reading to fall into place because students need to fully understand a text before they are ready to form an opinion about it.

The word *opinion* might be new to many of our young readers, so simply asking them to state their opinion might not garner the results we are looking for. First, we must teach students what an opinion is and what it means to have an opinion about something. I recommend a simple sentence, such as My opinion is what I think or feel about something. Morning meeting is a great time to introduce and practice simple opinions by asking a question like, In your opinion, what is the best show on TV? Even our youngest students have an opinion about that! The more we fold the language of close reading into other parts of our day, the more concrete that language and learning becomes for our students. Once students know what an opinion is, they are able to form opinions within close reading experiences.

To truly be close, critical readers, our students must not only be able to form opinions but also be able to support those opinions with text evidence. I know. There's nothing like the words *text evidence* to take the wind out of our primary-grade teacher sails. Opinions? We can do this! Text evidence? No thanks! The good news is, like any part of close reading with primary-grade students, we can make this a shared learning experience. By allowing our students to lean on us and on each other, we make the process of finding supporting evidence less stressful for us and more accessible for our students. Do not be afraid to form opinions as a class and make the process of returning to the text to find evidence a teacher-led but student-driven experience. Follow your students' thinking as you show them how to support their opinions with some not-so-scary text evidence.

A simple shared-writing opinion with evidence written with kindergarten students is shown in Figure 3.15, while Figure 3.16 shows a second-grade student's opinion with evidence after taking a closer look at the diagram at the end of *Giant Squid*. Keep in mind that opinions with evidence, especially for our youngest readers and writers, do not always have to be written. Speaking and listening opportunities are just as powerful as students work to make meaning from a text. If writing something down takes away from the intended purpose of the learning activity, switch it up and make it an opportunity for student discussion instead.

■ Questioning and Discussion for What the Text Means

Meaning making and arriving at big understandings are no easy tasks for young readers; however, the questions we pose and the discussion opportunities we provide assist students as they build their comprehension of a text. Questions that get students thinking about what a text means can have several focal points, many of which are outlined in earlier sections, but all of them are tied together under this meaning-making umbrella. Because meaning making is unique to each reader, responses to these questions will most likely not be of the cookie-cutter variety. Part of close reading is letting understanding unfold, with you facilitating instead of handing out the answers. When we are not seeking one correct answer or one correct understanding, and through the different lenses of individual readers, we shine the spotlight on student voices sharing the meanings they have created. Here are some questions that work well for discussing what a text may mean.

Figure 3.15
Shared writing opportunities are perfect for supporting little readers as they learn to provide evidence for their thinking.

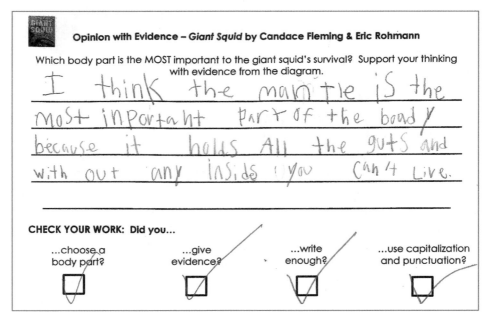

Figure 3.16
Second-grade students closely read the diagram in *Giant Squid* to determine importance and form an opinion.

TEXT-DEPENDENT QUESTIONS FOR WHAT THE TEXT MEANS	
FICTION	INFORMATIONAL
• How do the title and front cover help you understand this text? • What was the author thinking when he or she wrote this book? • Why did the illustrator choose to draw this picture for this page? • What do you know about the character(s)? How do you know these things? • What message is this book sending to you? What are the important parts along the way that led you to this message? • What is the most important thing you will take away from this book as a reader? • Do you think other kids should read this book? Why?	• How do the title and front cover help you understand this text? • What did the author want to teach us by writing this book? • How do the text features help you better understand the text? • How did you use what you already knew to help you as you read this text? • What is the main idea of this text? What were some important parts along the way that led you to this main idea? • What is the most important thing you learned from this book? • Do you think other kids should read this book? Why?

■ Annotation During a Third Reading Experience

In the later stages of close reading, we begin to think about annotation as a way for students to make meaning of the text as a whole. This might mean students use (or we use together) sticky notes to jot some new understandings that have come to them over the course of the close reading experience. It might also mean that students start to write down some of their wonderings or questions that have arisen or that are still lingering after reading a text.

As students work to craft the main idea or central message of a text, determining importance is crucial. An annotation technique that works well with young readers who are determining importance is placing little star stickers next to words, sentences, paragraphs, or pages that are essential to generating a big understanding. Students love stickers, and I love that it takes less time than teaching them how to draw a star! You've got to steal time where you can, and I choose to steal it from star making. Figure 3.17 shows a student putting the star stickers to work as he reads a short article about animal migration. Students use their star stickers to help them keep track of the important parts of a text before participating in collaborative conversations with peers.

Figure 3.17
A first-grade student uses star stickers to annotate the important parts of an article.

Text-to-text connections also make great annotations using the sentence frame This reminds me of . . . ." Students can jot down these notes themselves or create them during a shared annotating experience. The important thing to remember about annotating is that it should enhance understanding and encourage easy recall of previous thinking and learning within a close reading experience. Meaning-based annotations are an important step in the process of developing new literacy learning.

■ What Does the Text Inspire You to Do?

Okay, so we've read, reread, talked, and written about a text. Can we be done now? Not just yet—we're almost at the best part of close reading! Certainly it is tempting to read a book, get to the point, and move on quickly, especially with the growing demands for content coverage during the school day. But when we close the book and put it back on our shelf after figuring out what the text means, we can miss an amazing learning opportunity for our students. A final experience during a sequence of close reading lessons involves more than putting all the pieces of the text together. We ask ourselves, What is it about the message of this text that begs to be explored further, outside the text?

This part of close reading provides even more of a chance for us to learn about our students as readers and thinkers—what motivates, drives, and inspires them. During this phase of close reading the students really take ownership and showcase their understanding of a text with a culminating task or activity. Sometimes these culminating activities are teacher directed, meaning the students might be writing in response to a prompt or working in groups to answer a question or solve a problem related to the text. In other instances, students take complete ownership, diving into research to explore lingering questions or wonderings or taking action toward a goal inspired by their close reading experience. In any case, students work together, with you as the facilitator, to forge brand-new learning opportunities that highlight their big understandings from a text.

Text-inspired action can take the form of inquiry learning, social action, writing—any task derived from what they learned in a close reading experience. After using close reading strategies with *Pink Is for Blobfish*, my students had a good understanding of the text structure, the main idea, and the author's purpose for writing this book. When they were just as excited about this book on the fourth day as they were on the first day, I knew they were not done learning from it. I had planned a compare-and-contrast writing opportunity that I thought would allow them to showcase their thinking, but you know what they say about the best-laid plans. Then came Alex's question: "Is there gonna be a book for every color?" I admittedly did not know if there was going to be a book for every color, but never let them see you sweat! "That's a really great question, Alex! I'm not sure what Jess Keating's plans are, but I am thinking you just gave us an idea! Are your friends wondering about some other colors?" A unanimous "YES!" mixed with high-powered screaming (you know the kind) filled the room. One student's question sparked a whole-class inquiry experience as the group broke up into color teams and began researching animals that fit the color they chose. Their inquiry led them to more informational books, articles, and websites about animals. (Thank you, instructional technology people everywhere, for your expertise and patience with little researchers!) Students adopted the format of *Blobfish* as they created their own "color" animal books based on their new learning. This inquiry experience came straight from the students, but they needed that nudge from me to make it possible. As teachers we must be willing to follow the thinking and passions of our students, even if it means you won't get to move on to the next thing right away (see Figure 3.18).

Figure 3.18
Second-grade students researched different-color animals following a close reading experience.

When text-inspired action meets social action, we fuse literacy learning and social-emotional learning as students work to make a change or difference in some way. We know that educating students on the social-emotional level is becoming increasingly important, especially for our littlest learners. Empathy, acceptance, tolerance, and understanding do not always come naturally for most children. Our students must be taught and empowered to be agents of change in the classroom, in school, and in communities near and far. Never before has it been so important to amplify the voices and the thinking of our students—they need to know that they can be change-makers and that their ideas matter. Often students' inspiration to make a difference or call to action can blossom because of the close reading of a text, so it is crucial that we as teachers are mindful and deliberate about the texts we bring into close reading experiences. For example, after reading *The Smallest Girl in the Smallest Grade*, first-grade students were inspired to write letters and make posters to spread the word about the dangers of bullying and the power of standing up for one another. One student even wrote a short anti-bullying piece that she read for the whole school during morning announcements. This school-based social action arose because the students were inspired by the new understandings they took away from a close look at the book over multiple readings.

Another example of text-inspired action came after reading *One Plastic Bag*, when first-grade students were prompted by the book to think about how plastic and pollution can hurt people, animals, and plants. An insightful class discussion allowed even these young minds to think about their impact on the world around them. They thought about the ways they use plastic, what they do with plastic when they're done with it, and whether they could make better choices about plastic. Reflecting on this discussion and given time to think about how to make a difference, these first graders came up with some amazing ways to do their part. A few students wrote notes to their family members encouraging them to bring reusable bags to the stores they visit (some even used text evidence in their letters—oh yeah!). Many students made posters encouraging students to bring reusable water bottles to school instead of a new plastic one each day. Another group of students wanted to advocate for recycling bins for plastic because the bins we currently had in our school were only for paper. Some things were easier for students to accomplish than others, but the feeling of empower-ment and the ability to make a difference even at a young age stuck with them all year long.

These wonderings and sparks of inspiration do not always happen or come naturally for students. In a perfect world, our students would always ask the exact right questions at the exact right time, but we know that this is not always the case. It is easy to think, my students are not like that; this would never happen with my students. But understand that our belief in our young readers as big thinkers plays a key role in their belief in themselves and in their ability to ask the kinds of questions that steer their learning in new directions. We must not forget that our students need our support to guide them toward the kinds of questions and wonderings that culminate in learning. There are several instances during which I have nudged students' thinking a bit in order to take their thinking to the next level. Remember to nudge, but also remember to let learning unfold naturally after the nudge.

■ Moving Forward

With each reading of a text, we want to delve a little further into the minds of our young readers, pulling out and nurturing the great thinking we know is in there. Think about the students with whom you work every day. What texts or topics excite them? What are their reading goals? What close reading opportunities can you provide them with that will take their basic understanding and allow it to develop into a deep comprehension that they can transfer to other texts and other learning experiences? The close reading experiences presented in this chapter are meant to guide your thinking as you navigate the many components of close reading and the many routes that close reading can take. No close reading experience is as neat and tidy in real life as it looks in a book (especially with primary-grade students), but it is my belief that these ideas—combined with your expertise—will move your young readers forward.

4

Inside the Classroom: Close Reading Texts and Lessons

One day, the girl has a wonderful idea. She is going to make the most MAGNIFICENT thing! She knows just how it will look. She knows just how it will work. All she has to do is make it, and she makes things all the time. Easy-peasy!
—ASHLEY SPIRES, *THE MOST MAGNIFICENT THING*

One of the trickiest yet most rewarding parts of close reading is figuring out how all your instruction will come together. What should students do first? Where exactly does this piece fit? Should we annotate this text? What is the big idea here? Is this the best text for what we're trying to accomplish? It is exciting to see all the pieces of the close reading puzzle start to fit into a sequence that makes sense for you and for the little readers you teach. However, the puzzle pieces do not always fit together in the same way for each close reading experience you will engage in with your students.

This chapter is devoted to sharing close reading lesson ideas that have worked for the students with whom I spend my teaching time. I have included seven examples of close reading sequences that range from kindergarten through second grade to serve as models or mentor texts as you design learning experiences that meet the needs of your young readers.

These lesson outlines are based on literary and informational texts as well as song lyrics, and they include target standards, descriptions of the learning experiences, possible text-dependent questions for discussion, and examples of student work. Keep in mind that there is no magic close reading sequence that will work with every teacher, every student, or in every classroom (Although that would be nice, wouldn't it?). Close reading is so much more than read, annotate, ask text-dependent questions, repeat, yet it is very tempting to fall into this easy sequence. I get it. We're teachers. We like a good system. But we must also trust ourselves enough to be able to diverge from the appealing routine and dive into something a little more creative and relevant for our students. You plan amazing and innovative learning experiences for your students each day—you do it all the time! Planning for close reading is no different. And although it might not be Pinterest-perfect from the start (or ever), the possibilities for learning will be far-reaching.

To plan meaningful close reading opportunities, we must first know our students as readers, writers, and thinkers. The lessons included in this chapter are meant to serve as a guide—not a formula—for what close reading might look like as you engage in it with your young readers. To use Fisher and Frey's words, treat these sample close reading lessons as "a tool for organizing the journey through a piece of text," rather than cookie-cutter templates to be filled in (2014b, 7). Bearing in mind that your students' natural inquisitiveness and love of reading will organically prompt some of your best close reading experiences, allow yourself to use these lesson ideas as mentor texts for crafting meaningful close reading journeys of your own. My hope is that some of my ideas will work in your classroom and inspire you to plan and share close reading lessons of your own.

Earlier in this book I wrote about the importance of connecting the learning that takes place during a close reading experience to the reading that students are doing independently. When you are planning for close reading in your classroom, don't forget about your little readers. Christopher Lehman and Kate Roberts say it perfectly in *Falling in Love with Close Reading*: "Powerful close reading instruction must be designed in response to the strengths and needs of your students, not planned solely to match a book or fit a scope and sequence" (2014, 5). So, think first about your students. Then think about texts and reading experiences that will match the goals or outcomes you have for them. What kinds of things are your students coming across in the books they are able to read on their own? How will your close reading plans reflect your students' lives and cultures, as well as what they need right now as readers? Anticipate using close reading in a way that will allow for transference from a text you read together to the texts that students are reading independently. Think about what aspects of close reading will move your students forward as a community of readers.

Finally, let us not forget the value of collaboration when planning opportunities for our students to engage deeply with texts. I am a firm believer that we can do good thinking alone, but we can do great thinking together with our colleagues. Some of my best close reading lesson ideas have arisen from conversations with other teachers as they've helped me choose the right text, noodled with me about a crazy idea, or simply shared what's worked for them. In a world where competition is often praised and the quest to be the best is tempting, we must not lose sight of the power of collaboration. The more we share as teachers, the more our students learn. Think of me as your teammate from afar, supporting you and cheering you on every step of the way. Planning for close reading is no easy task, but I believe in teachers; I believe in you.

GRADE LEVEL: KINDERGARTEN
TEXT: *RECESS AT 20 BELOW* BY CINDY LOU AILLAUD
Background Information: This close reading experience arose out of the need to deepen student learning and understanding during a unit on winter. My students were able to recall basic facts about winter, like "It's cold" or "It snows," but were not doing much thinking beyond these general ideas. I wanted them to know what winter is like, but they already knew that–they didn't need me to tell them. We began to look beyond what we already knew about winter to what winter is like outside our chilly, gray city. We love you, Chicago, but sometimes you are just too cold. *Recess at 20 Below* is a text that had everything I was looking for. It is an informational text that has complex vocabulary yet connects with students. It also provides young readers with a window to the world as they learn about children's lives that are different from their own.
First Experience Common Core State Standards (CCSS): CCSS.ELA-Literacy.RI.K.1, K.10 • Introduce *Recess at 20 Below* by telling students that today they will be reading and learning about a place in America that has really cold winters–even colder than ours! Read the title aloud to students and have a brief discussion about the location of Alaska and what "20 below" means. You can also ask students, "What happens here at our school when it gets really cold? Do we go outside for recess?" Allow students time to answer before telling them that kids in Alaska go outside for recess, even when it is super cold! "Today we will read about how those kids get ready for recess and what they do once they are outside. Some things might be the same as what you kids do, but other things are very different. Let's read about this exciting and cold place!"

- Read the book aloud, pausing for discussion at necessary places. Students will probably have a lot to say about this book, which is great because you will be using this text for several reading experiences. Provide students with turn-and-talk opportunities as they answer some text-dependent questions for general understanding. Listen in on student conversations to take the pulse of student understanding during and after this first reading.

- Possible Text-Dependent Questions for Discussion

  ○ What is this book about?

  ○ Where do the kids live?

  ○ What kinds of things do the kids wear for recess?

  ○ What do the kids do at recess?

  ○ Why are the kids not able to use some of their outside toys at recess?

- Share Your Thinking

  ○ To capture their thinking from this first reading, students will draw and/ or write their thinking in their reader's notebooks or on a given Share Your Thinking page such as the one in Appendix A. They may then participate in a partner or small-group discussion as students share their initial thinking with one another.

Second Experience
CCSS: CCSS.ELA-Literacy.RI.K.4, K.10

- During this second experience with the text, tell students that instead of reading the whole book, you are just going to read and work with a few pages. Before beginning, ask students to recall and share some of the facts from the previous reading that they learned about recess in Alaska. Invite them to bring their notebooks to the rug to review and share the thinking they recorded during the first reading experience.

- Today students will be listening for a few new words and trying to figure out the meaning of those words using guidance and support from you (the teacher) and context clues from the text.

- Before reading, tell students the vocabulary words they will be listening for on each page. Invite them to listen carefully for the words because the class will discuss what those words mean after the page has been read. After reading the page(s) that contain the new vocabulary words, draw the students' attention to their Word Detective chart (created before the lesson, example follows; see Appendix D for a blank chart form that students can use alongside the whole-class chart if desired) on which the words will be defined. The class will work together, using prior knowledge, context clues, or other strategies to arrive at the meaning of the new words.

WORD	WHAT DO WE THINK IT MEANS?	WHAT DOES IT REALLY MEAN?	HOW DO WE KNOW? WHAT MAKES US THINK THAT?
Wading			
Parka			
Glacier			

- Possible Text-Dependent Questions for Discussion

  ○ How does this word help you understand what's happening on this page?

  ○ How did the author help us figure out what this word meant?

  ○ Why does this word work well here?

  ○ How did you figure out the meaning of this word?

- After class discussion of text-dependent questions and completion of the vocabulary table, students may choose one of the new words to add to their word detective journals (see Appendix E). They may also add the words to your content-area word wall or wherever you display content-area learning in your classroom.

Third Experience

CCSS: CCSS.ELA-Literacy.RI.K.2, K.10; CCSS.ELA-Literacy.SL.K.1a, K.2

- Take a picture-walk through the book, calling attention to important parts of the text and reading aloud only some parts to refresh students' memories. Today you are going to guide students as they determine key words from a few of the book's pages in order to help them form the main idea of the text.

- Start by telling students that you are going to be looking closely at a few pages of the book in order to decide on the key words. In other words, what is/are the most important word(s) on each page? Decide which four or five pages you deem important because they contribute heavily to the main idea of the text. Read these pages aloud to students one at time. After reading each page, ask, Which word on this page tells us the most about the page? Or, Which word on the page do you think is really important to helping us understand? Allow students time to share with a partner or two before they share their ideas with the whole class. Record their word(s) on the board or on your chart paper under the heading Key Words. Repeat this process for three or four more pages so that you have a total of four to five key words from which to create your main idea. Following are some possible key words your students might notice. Annotate these key words with Wikki Stix to show their importance. (See Figure 4.1.)

Figure 4.1
A small group of kindergarten readers takes a closer look at important words from *Recess at 20 Below*.

Page 2 – cold
Page 3 - recess
Page 7 – clothes
Page 8 – outside
Page 19 – freeze
Page 29 – mess

- After you have listed your key words, tell students that when we read nonfiction, key words help us to arrive at the main idea of the text. If needed, remind students what the main idea of the text is. "How can we use these key words to help us figure out what the text is mostly about?" Think aloud as you repeat the key words to students and allow them the opportunity to turn and talk with one another to come up with what the text is mostly about. Guide students as they share their answers and you form a main idea together. An example of a main idea using some of the key words might be, "The main idea of the book is that kids in Alaska go outside for recess even when it is really, really freezing." Or, "The main idea of the book is that kids in Alaska have a unique recess experience."
- As a shared/guided writing experience, write the main idea of the text on chart paper to use during subsequent readings.

Fourth Experience

CCSS: CCSS.ELA-Literacy.RI.K.2, K.10; CCSS.ELA-Literacy.SL.K.1a, K.2

- Begin today's session by reviewing the main idea that you created together during the previous reading. Today students will focus on details from the book. It might be helpful to compare details to the main idea. Remind students, While the main idea is the "big picture," what the book is mostly about, the details are all of the little pieces of information that we learned along the way. Read and review the main idea once more before inviting students to help with the details. Allow time for students to talk with one another before sharing out their details. As students share their details, add them to your chart.

- Once you are finished adding and discussing details, reiterate for students once again the difference between the main idea and details. The main idea means the overall message or what the book is mostly about, and the details are all the little pieces of information the story contains that support the main idea.

- Use student-generated details as a quick-check assessment of understanding. (See Figure 4.2.)

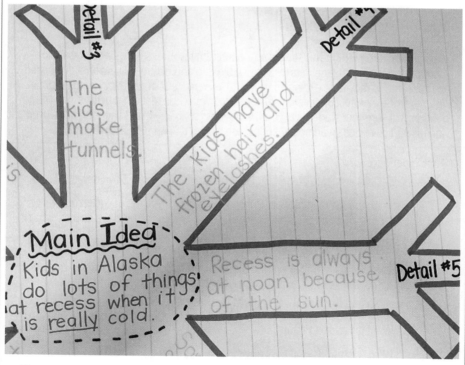

Figure 4.2

A close-up of this chart shows student thinking about the main idea and details from *Recess at 20 Below*.

Fifth Experience and Culminating Task

CCSS: CCSS.ELA-Literacy.RI.K.1., K.2, K.10; CCSS.ELA-Literacy.SL.K.1a, K.2

- Use this fifth reading to reflect on the learning you have gained up until this point. Remind students about informational text, the new vocabulary learned, and main idea and details. Today the focus will be on student wonderings that will lead to future inquiry learning. What do your students still want to know about recess or the kids in Alaska? If desired, students can write or draw a response to an "I'm wondering . . . " sentence in their notebooks or on a small sheet of paper with the sentence frame "I'm wondering . . ." at the top. Or, you can choose to record their wonderings on the board or on chart paper. Student questions and wonderings can be used as a launching point for inquiry learning during future reading workshop time.

- Writing Extension Activity: Using *Recess at 20 Below* as a mentor text, students may create a class book that teaches about the characteristics of wintertime recess where they live.

GRADE LEVEL: KINDERGARTEN

TEXT: "I AM A PIZZA" SONG LYRICS

Background Information: This song is a kindergarten favorite! Its lyrics also present lots of opportunities for little readers to do some big thinking. Students were already hooked on the song, so they were eager to dive in and learn more about it. Using song lyrics can often provide a perfect opportunity to ease into some close reading practices with young readers. I'm sure your students have a favorite class song–try it out! The song lyrics used for this particular close reading experience are included in Appendix F of this book.

First Experience

CCSS: CCSS.ELA-Literacy.RF.K.1, CCSS.ELA-Literacy.RL.K.1, CCSS.ELA-Literacy.SL.K.2

- Listen to the song and follow along with the lyrics you have written on chart paper or typed up for students. Read the lyrics together and create a thinking trail (see Chapter 2 and Appendix A) to keep track of student thinking about the events that are taking place during each verse of the song. (See Figure 4.3.)

- Invite students to find and annotate each letter *P* or *p* that appears in the lyrics. Students may also find and annotate any pertinent sight words, such as *was* or *of*.

- Possible Text-Dependent Questions for Discussion

  - What is this song about?

  - Who is doing the talking? Are there any other characters?

  - What toppings did the pizza have?

  - What happened to the pizza?

Figure 4.3
Printing the song lyrics on a poster or chart paper allows for whole-group annotation that helps students keep track of their thinking.

Second Experience
CCSS: CCSS.ELA-Literacy.RF.K.2

- Prior to the second reading of this text, review student thinking from the previous session, and ask readers to share what they remember about the song lyrics. This is a good time to recycle the text-dependent questions (TDQs) from the first session, allowing them to serve as a launching point for this session's learning. The second reading of these lyrics will focus on the organization and sequence of the events of the song so that students are able to understand and retell the story that takes place within the lyrics.

- Listen to the song again, and read the lyrics aloud for students. Refer to the thinking trail you created during the last session to help students remember each verse. Use directed drawing to create simple sequencing cards that students can use as they practice retelling the story. Introduce or review some basic transition words—first, next, then, after that—to help students move their retellings along. Invite students to sequence their cards and retell the story of the song with a partner. Listen in on students as they retell the story in order to capture a snapshot of understanding.

- Possible Text-Dependent Questions for Discussion

  ○ How is the song organized?

  ○ Do you notice any patterns in the lyrics? Why do you think the songwriter did that?

  ○ What is different about the last verse of the song? How does that help you understand the song?

- Connection to Independent Learning: Invite students to create and use their own sequence and retelling cards for their independent reading books or favorite stories that have been read to them.

Third Experience
CCSS: CCSS.ELA-Literacy.RL.K.3

- Digging deeper into the song lyrics, this reading will focus on identifying characters and drawing inferences about them. Inferring can be a tricky comprehension skill for young readers, so building it in to a close reading experience is helpful because students have become very familiar with the text. Begin this session by listening to the song and reading the lyrics again with students.

- Ask students to determine who the characters are in the song. The main character, the pizza, will be more obvious to them than the implied character—the pizza delivery person. Discuss the idea of an implied character and invite students to share how they know there is another character in the song even though the lyrics don't directly state that this is the case. Annotate the chart-paper copy of the lyrics to show student thinking throughout this discussion.

- Invite students to share what they know about each character. Teach them that when they can figure something out about a character or a story without having the author directly tell them in the text, it is called inferring. As students share their ideas about each character, challenge them to defend their thinking and provide evidence by asking, *How do you know?*
- Possible Text-Dependent Questions for Discussion

  - What do you know about the characters?

  - How does the songwriter give us clues about the pizza delivery person?

  - How did the pizza change from the beginning of the song to the end?

Writing Extension

- Using "I Am a Pizza" as a mentor text, compose a companion song that follows a similar sequence. This can be a whole-class, shared writing experience, or students can try it out for themselves in their notebooks. Some favorite companion song ideas from my students include "I Am a Donut" and "I Am a Butterfly." (See Figure 4.4.)

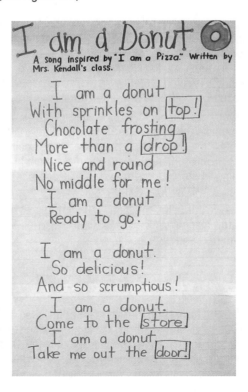

Figure 4.4
This companion song was composed during a shared writing experience that followed a close reading of "I am a Pizza" song lyrics.

GRADE LEVEL: FIRST GRADE
TEXT: *PINK IS FOR BLOBFISH* BY JESS KEATING AND DAVID DEGRAND (ILLUSTRATOR)

Background Information: Keating and DeGrand's informational books beg to be read again and again. This particular book fits in nicely with a first-grade unit on animals and their habitats.

First Experience

CCSS: CCSS.ELA-Literacy.RI.1.1, 1.10

- Create relevance for students by using the Possible Sentences (Beers and Probst 2015) strategy. Provide students with a list of words and phrases that appear in the book. Choose a few pages to focus on (the book is lengthy), and pull your words and phrases from those pages. With first graders, it is helpful to choose ten to fifteen words–enough so they can create some sentences, but not so many as to overwhelm them. Ask students to think about some of the words in the list that might go together, allowing time for turn-and-talk conversations with peers. Create some sentences from the list as a class that students think might appear in the pages they are about to read.

- Read aloud the chosen pages of the book, reminding students to listen for the words and phrases in the Possible Sentences word bank that were used to create your initial sentences. Tell them they are reading to monitor whether their thinking is correct and to gather information in order to create new sentences or revise existing sentences to make them correct. Use whole-class annotation to mark some of the words and phrases as they appear in the context of the text.

- Revisit the sentences the class created before reading, marking them as TRUE if evidence from the reading supports the sentence as being true. Work with students to revise any sentences in order to make them true based on evidence from the reading. Invite students to share the evidence they are using to revise their sentences. Ask, How do you know that?

- Nudge students to notice the similarities and differences between their before-reading and after-reading sentences. Facilitate a discussion that requires students to compare and contrast the two.

Second Experience

CCSS: CCSS.ELA-Literacy.RI.1.5

- This second session focuses on the text features included in the book. Choose two or three double-page spreads to read aloud, asking students to notice similarities in structure on each animal's pages. Work together to name and label those text features. Use guided or shared annotation to label each text feature with its name and to discuss each feature's function.

- Possible Text-Dependent Questions for Discussion

  ○ What text features are you noticing on each page?

- ○ Why do you think the text is organized in this way?

- ○ How do the text features on each page work together?

- ○ How is the paragraph at the top different from the fun fact underneath it? How does that help you as a reader?

- ○ Why are the quick facts on the side important?

- ○ Can you think of other ways to organize this text?

Third Experience
CCSS: CCSS.ELA-Literacy.RI.1.2

- Focus on and read aloud another two or three double-page spreads for this third session. Introduce or review the concept of main topic and key details, telling students that they will be using what they know about the contents of this book so far to think about the author's purpose.
- Possible Text-Dependent Questions for Discussion

  - ○ What is the main topic of this book/page?

  - ○ How were you able to determine the main topic?

  - ○ What is the main thing the author is trying to teach us with this book/page?

- Send students off in partnerships or small groups to think together about the book's main topic and some of the key details it presents. Allow them to record their thinking using their notebooks or a graphic organizer of some kind. Bring students together after a few minutes to share their thinking with the whole class. Record their thinking on the board or chart paper.
- Using student thinking about main topic and key details, participate in a shared writing experience that explains the author's purpose. Invite students to explain the author's purpose to their peers following the shared writing experience. Listen in on student conversations for a quick-check assessment of understanding.

Fourth Experience and Culminating Task
CCSS: CCSS.ELA-Literacy.RI.1.1

- Look closely at the double-page spread for just one animal. Invite students to notice the information that the author includes. Keep a list of the kinds of facts that fit into a book like this (quick facts for diet, habitat, etc.; obscure facts; interesting pieces about the animal's life, survival, etc.).

- Possible Text-Dependent Questions for Discussion

  ○ Why do you think the author included these kinds of facts?

  ○ How can we use this information to conduct our own research?

- Inquiry Research: Allow students to work in teams to conduct research on animals of different colors. Guide them first to research and make a list of a few animals that are the color they chose (blue, green, yellow, etc.), then send them off to find specific information about each animal on their list. Challenge them to think like the author as they are gathering their information. This experience will span several class periods, but you'll find the results to be well worth the time!

GRADE LEVEL: FIRST GRADE

TEXT: *THE SMALLEST GIRL IN THE SMALLEST GRADE* BY JUSTIN ROBERTS AND CHRISTIAN ROBINSON (ILLUSTRATOR)

Background Information: This text is perfect for close reading at the beginning of the year when establishing what's important to your classroom community.

First Experience

CCSS: CCSS.ELA-Literacy.RL.1.1, 1.2

- Briefly introduce the story by reading the title and asking students to look closely at the front cover. What do they notice? What might this story be about?
- Read the book aloud, pausing minimally for discussion yet ensuring that students are following the story.
- Following reading, use the basic elements of the story to invite students to summarize and retell using the Somebody Wanted But So strategy (SWBS) (Macon, Bewell, and Vogt 1991), in which students answer questions related to words *somebody, wanted, but,* and *so* as described in Chapter 3. (See Figure 4.5.)
- Possible Text-Dependent Questions for Discussion

  ○ Who is the main character (Somebody)?

  ○ What do you learn about Sally from this book?

  ○ Where does the story take place?

  ○ What did Sally notice (Wanted)?

  ○ What was the problem in the story (But)? How do you learn about the problem?

  ○ Why did the school transform (So)?

Figure 4.5
This completed chart shows students' initial understanding of *The Smallest Girl in the Smallest Grade* using the Somebody Wanted But So strategy.

Second Experience

CCSS: CCSS.ELA-Literacy.RL.1.4

- During this second experience with the text, tell students that instead of reading the whole book, you are just going to read and work with a few pages. Before beginning, ask students to recall and retell the story with a partner, leaning on the SWBS strategy from the previous session.

Note: This session is split into two parts and may take more than one class session to complete.

- PART ONE: As the selected pages for this session are read aloud, students will be listening for a new word on each page, trying to figure out the meaning of the word using guidance and support from you (the teacher), context clues from the text, and any information they may hold in their schema.

- Before reading, tell students the vocabulary words they will be listening for on each page. Invite them to listen carefully for the words because the class will discuss what those words mean after the page has been read. After reading the page(s) that contain the new vocabulary words, draw the students' attention to the chart (created before the lesson and using the version of the I Am a Word Detective chart that follows) on which the words will be defined. The class will work together, using prior knowledge, context clues, or other strategies to arrive at the meaning of the new words.

NEW WORD	WHAT DO WE THINK IT MEANS?	WHAT DOES IT REALLY MEAN?	HOW DO WE KNOW? WHAT MAKES US THINK THAT?
continue			
abandoned			
cower			
transform			

- Possible Text-Dependent Questions for Discussion

  ○ How does this word help you understand what's happening on this page?

  ○ How did the author help us figure out what this word meant?

  ○ Why does this word work well here?

  ○ How did you figure out the meaning of this word?

- Following a class discussion of text-dependent questions and completion of the vocabulary table, students may choose one of the new words to add to their word detective journals (see Appendix E). They may also add the words to your content-area word wall or wherever you display content-area learning in your classroom. (See Figure 4.6.)

Figure 4.6
This first-grade student's word detective journal shows her understanding of the word *transform*.

- PART TWO: In addition to looking at the interesting vocabulary the author used, students will also want to look closely at the figurative language used throughout the story. Here are some sentences worth calling their attention to.

  - She'd seen how a whisper could make someone cower, **like a bulldozer crushing** through fields of wildflowers.

  - **Like waves rolling in,** one after another, first Molly rose up, then Michael's twin brother.

  - . . . they all felt, for a moment, **like the janitor's keys.** Fastened together with a heavy steel ring that held all the secrets to unlock everything.

- Allow students to share their thinking about the meaning of these special sentences. Invite them to also think of the author's purpose for using words and phrases such as these. Record student thinking on the board or on a chart to make the learning visible and to allow these sentences to serve as mentors when students are looking to include some powerful words and phrases in their own writing.

- Possible Text-Dependent Questions for Discussion

  - Why do you think the author chose to use these words and phrases?

  - What do these sentences do for us as readers?

  - Can we think of other ways to write these sentences?

  - How can we use sentences like this in our own writing?

Third Experience
CCSS: CCSS.ELA-Literacy.RF.1.1., CCSS.ELS-Literacy.SL.1.1

- Read the story aloud once again to begin this third session. Use a favorite speaking and listening strategy to engage students in discussion. I like using Keep the Line Alive (Serravallo 2015) or Inside-Outside Circle (Kagan and Kagan 2015). Allow student thinking to fuel the discussion, posing text-dependent questions to nudge students to some deeper understandings. Discussion during this reading of the text will focus on author's purpose as well as providing evidence to support thinking. (See Figure 4.7.)

- Possible Text-Dependent Questions

  - How was Sally able to transform her school?

  - Why do you think Justin Roberts wrote this book?

  - How did the school change at the end of the story? How do you know?

  - What message does this book send to us as first graders? What can we as first graders do now that we have read this story?

Figure 4.7
Students participating in a collaborative conversation using the Keep the Line Alive strategy.

- Text-Inspired Action: Invite students to share ideas for what they can do as first graders after spending some time with this text. What has this text taught them that they can take forward in the classroom, school, or community? Do they see ways to help make a change like Sally did in the story? Allow time for students to develop "action plans," and guide them as they work toward making a difference.

GRADE LEVEL: FIRST GRADE
TEXT: *JABARI JUMPS* BY GAIA CORNWALL

Background Information: This picture book is about gathering the courage to face big fears. It is a great text to read just before summer vacation begins.

First Experience

CCSS: CCSS.ELA-Literacy.RL.1.1, 1.2 CCSS.ELA-Literacy.RF.1.3e

- Briefly introduce the story by reading the title and asking students to look closely at the front cover. What do they notice? What might this story be about?
- Read the book aloud, pausing minimally for discussion yet ensuring students are following the story.
- Possible Text-Dependent Questions for Discussion

  ○ Who is the main character? Are there any supporting characters?

- Where does the story take place?

- What is the problem in the story? Does it get solved?

- How does Jabari overcome his fear?

- Why did the school transform?

- Following reading, invite students to use retell bracelets–small bracelets made from one pipe cleaner and five or six small beads that indicate the different parts of a story (first, next, then, after that, etc.)–to orally retell the story to a partner. Be sure they touch and slide each bead on the bracelet as they talk about each part of the story. Model this strategy in a shared retelling experience if needed before sending students off to try on their own. Teach students that readers often retell a story when a friend asks them, What happens in this story?

- Exploring Syllables: Gather students back together for an embedded foundational skills lesson using words from the story. Choose a sampling of words from the story that range from one to three syllables. Put each word on a note card or sentence strip, and invite students to sort the words into syllable-count categories. After sorting, add the words to a class chart and zoom in on the words with two syllables. Teach or reinforce how to chunk words into parts for quick and easy decoding. During independent reading, invite students to read closely in order to be able to add some of their own words to the syllable sort. Celebrate and share the new words added.

JABARI JUMPS – SYLLABLE WORK		
1 SYLLABLE	2 SYLLABLES	3 SYLLABLES
jump test climb down breath board up	diving before ladder something surprise began whisper flying jumper backflip	Jabari tomorrow remember together important

Second Experience

CCSS: CCSS.ELA-Literacy.RL.1.4

- Break the story into two parts, before the jump and after the jump. Introduce and read the story up to the page with the aerial view of Jabari on the diving board that says, "His toes curled around the rough edge." Pause here and have students discuss how Jabari might be feeling and how he has felt in the story up to this point, then have them share. Most likely, students will answer "scared" or "nervous." Record that thinking on a chart: Jabari is nervous. Then tell students that you are going to read this part of the story one more time, but that this time they are going to be really close listeners and close watchers to pick out some words, groups of words, or illustrations that show he is nervous. *When we hear words that show Jabari is nervous, we are going to stop to talk about them and record them on our chart.* Reread the story, inviting students to initiate pauses for discussion of words, phrases, and illustrations that contribute to Jabari's feeling of nervousness or fright. When you get to the page with the aerial view of the diving board, stop to discuss all the words that students have collected, and teach them that authors use words in special ways to show feelings. *Look at all the ways Gaia Cornwall showed us that Jabari was nervous!*

- Continue reading the rest of the story, then talk about how Jabari was feeling after the jump. Record that thinking on the chart: *Jabari is proud/happy/elated*, etc. Reread the second part of the book (after the jump), and repeat the process of looking for words, phrases, and illustrations that contribute to his happier feelings. (See Figures 4.8 and 4.9.)

- Possible Text-Dependent Questions for Discussion

  - How does Jabari feel during this part of the story? How do you know?

  - What does Gaia Cornwall do to create the mood of the story?

  - How do the words and pictures in the story work together? Let's look for examples together.

- Close the learning by teaching students that they just found evidence to support their thinking. Tell them that readers use clues in the words and pictures to show how they know something, and that is just what they did! Refer to or create a chart or poster that contains the definition of evidence.

- A possible quick-check assessment is a written response from students in their reader's/writer's notebooks. *Write one sentence that tells about how Jabari was feeling in the story. See if you can use a word or picture clue in your sentence. Draw a picture to go with your sentence.* Support students with scaffolds as needed.

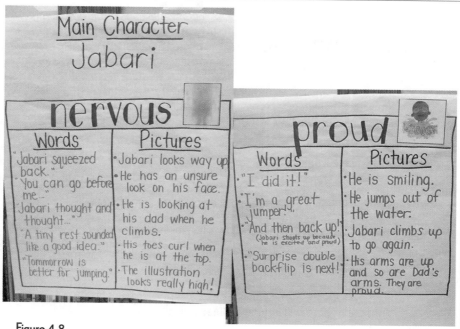

Figure 4.8
This chart shows the text evidence students gathered to support their thinking that Jabari was nervous before his jump.

Figure 4.9
At the end of the story, students noticed a shift in Jabari's feelings and used more text evidence to support their claim that Jabari was now feeling proud instead of nervous.

Third Experience and Culminating Task

CCSS: CCSS.ELA-Literacy.RF.1.1, 1.2; CCSS.ELA-Literacy.W.1.3

- Read the story again then take a picture-walk, or invite students to retell it with a partner before jumping into discussion questions.

- Possible Text-Dependent Questions for Discussion

    ○ Why do you think Gaia Cornwall wrote this book? What did she want us to know?

    ○ What are some ways that this book helps you as a first grader?

    ○ How can you use what you learned from this book to help others?

- Facilitate a discussion about the central message of this book. What is this book teaching us? Invite students to share their central message ideas on sticky notes, and place them on the central message chart you have created.

- Use the thinking that arises from the discussion questions to follow students' ideas about how they can use this text to help others. One idea is to create books for kindergarten students (next year's first graders) that will help them to not be scared or nervous when they get to first grade. *What stories could we tell or information could we give that will comfort the students coming to first grade next year and let them know that they will be okay?* Encourage students to draw from the different genres or formats that you have explored in reading and writing workshop throughout the year in order to craft their pieces. Some suggestions include

  - Write about a time in first grade when you felt scared or nervous, but everything turned out okay.

  - Write a question-and-answer book that teaches about first grade.

  - Write a story with a first-grade character who is courageous.

  - Use the structure of *Fortunately, Unfortunately* by Michael Foreman (2011) to write a book that will help new first graders.

  - Compose a wordless picture book or graphic novel about first grade. Challenge yourself to include a courageous character.

- Plan time for students to share their books with kindergarten students toward the end of the year.

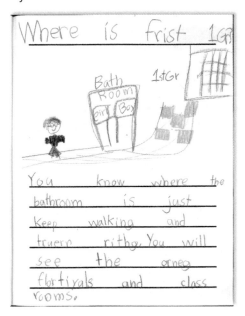

Figure 4.10
A first-grade student writes a question-and-answer book for kindergartners making the transition to first grade.

GRADE LEVEL: SECOND GRADE

TEXT: *GIANT SQUID* BY CANDACE FLEMING AND ERIC ROHMANN (ILLUSTRATOR)

Background Information: This book fits perfectly inside a unit on animals or animal habitats. With so much to notice and examine in both the words and the illustrations, close reading strategies are a must for complete understanding.

First Experience

CCSS: CCSS.ELA-Literacy R1.2.1, 2.10

- Create relevance for students by using the Possible Sentences (Beers and Probst 2015) strategy. Provide students with a list of fifteen to twenty words and phrases that appear in the book. Students will use these words and phrases to write two or three sentences they believe they might possibly see in the text. Challenge them to include at least three of the words/phrases from the word list in each sentence. Provide appropriate scaffolds for students if needed.

- Read the book aloud, reminding students to listen for the words and phrases in the possible sentences word bank. Tell them they are reading to monitor whether their thinking is correct and to learn information in order to create new sentences or revise existing sentences to make them correct. Use whole-class annotation to mark some of the words and phrases as they appear in the context of the text.

- After reading, students will revisit the sentences they created before reading, marking them as TRUE if evidence from the reading supports the sentence as being true, or revising their initial sentences in order to make them true based on evidence from the reading. Invite students to share the evidence they are using to revise their sentences. Ask, How do you know that?

- Nudge students to notice the similarities and differences between their before-reading and after-reading sentences. Facilitate a discussion that requires students to compare and contrast the two.

- Possible Text-Dependent Questions for Discussion

  ○ Why is the giant squid so mysterious?

  ○ What do you know about the giant squid's appearance?

  ○ How does the giant squid catch its prey?

  ○ Where does the giant squid live?

Second Experience

CCSS: CCSS.ELA-Literacy.RI.2.2

- This second session with *Giant Squid* focuses on determining main ideas and key details. Students will work in small groups to sort words and phrases from the text to help them think about and synthesize main ideas and key details.

- Provide students with an assortment of words and phrases from the text. It works well to use small sticky notes for the words and phrases so students can manipulate and sort them easily. (See Figure 4.11.) Students will work in their small groups to sort the words/phrases from the text according to a common theme or category. For example, a group might be thinking that certain words all seem to be about what the giant squid looks like, so they would group those together. That same group might also notice that a group of words goes together because they are all enemies of the giant squid. Students can sort their words however they see fit, but they should be able to explain their reasoning. (See Figure 4.12.) Once all words and phrases have been sorted into groups or categories, students should give each group a heading, such as habitat, appearance, diet, etc. (See Figure 4.13.)

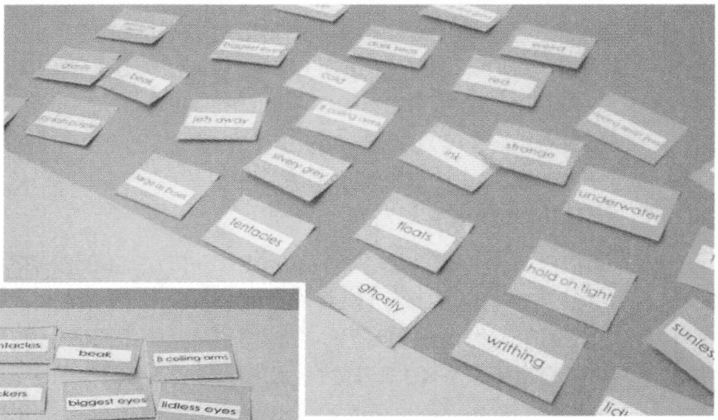

Figure 4.11
An assortment of words and phrases from *Giant Squid*

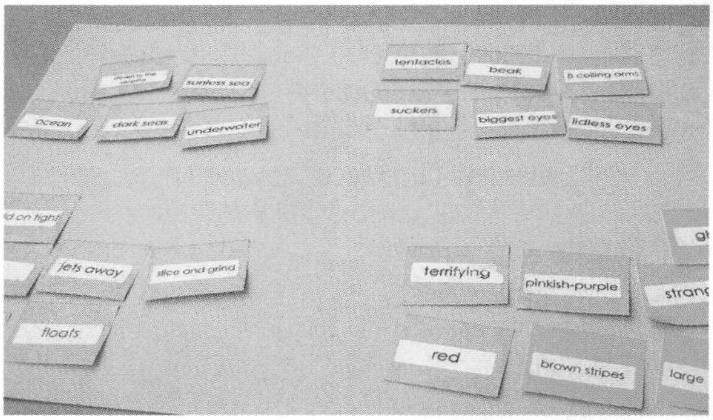

Figure 4.12
Students sort words and phrases into categories.

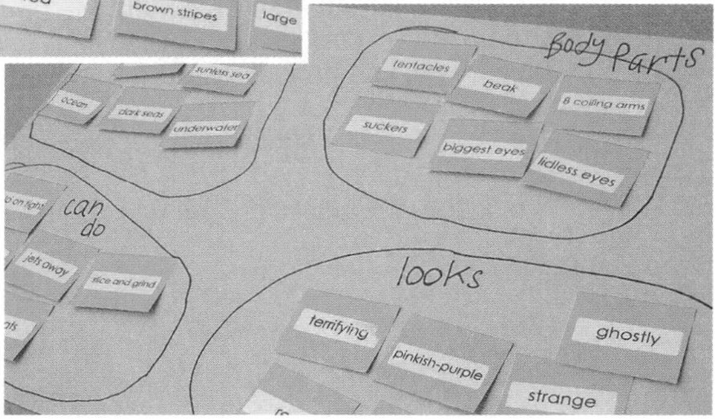

Figure 4.13
Students use commonalities between sorted words to create headings for each category.

○ NOTE: It may be helpful to differentiate the sorting experience for students. While some students might be able to group and categorize the words/ phrases on their own without the support of a category heading (called an open sort), other students may need the scaffold of provided category headings to use when grouping the words/phrases (a closed sort). (See Figures 4.14 and 4.15.)

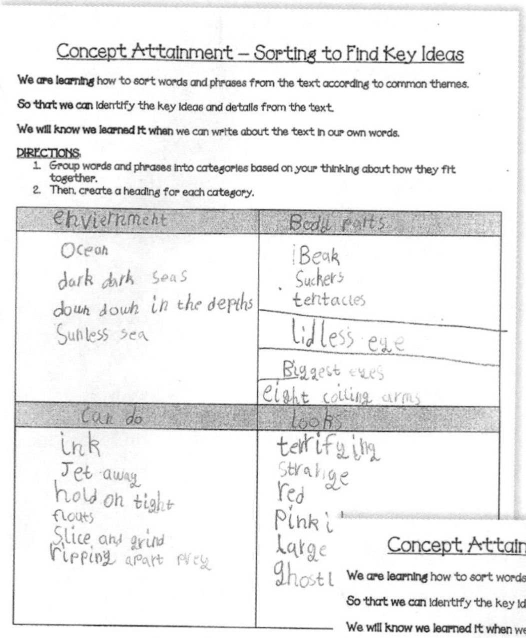

Concept Attainment – Sorting to Find Key Ideas

We are learning how to sort words and phrases from the text according to common themes.

So that we can identify the key ideas and details from the text.

We will know we learned it when we can write about the text in our own words.

DIRECTIONS:
1. Group words and phrases into categories based on your thinking about how they fit together.
2. Then, create a heading for each category.

envieriment	Body parts
Ocean	Beak
dark dark Seas	Suckers
down down in the depths	tentacles
Sunless sea	Lidless eye
	Biggest eyes
	eight coiling arms

Can do	Look
ink	terrifying
Jet away	strange
hold on tight	red
floats	Pink
Slice and grind	Large
ripping apart prey	ghostl

Figure 4.14
Students record their sorting work to help them think further about key ideas and details.

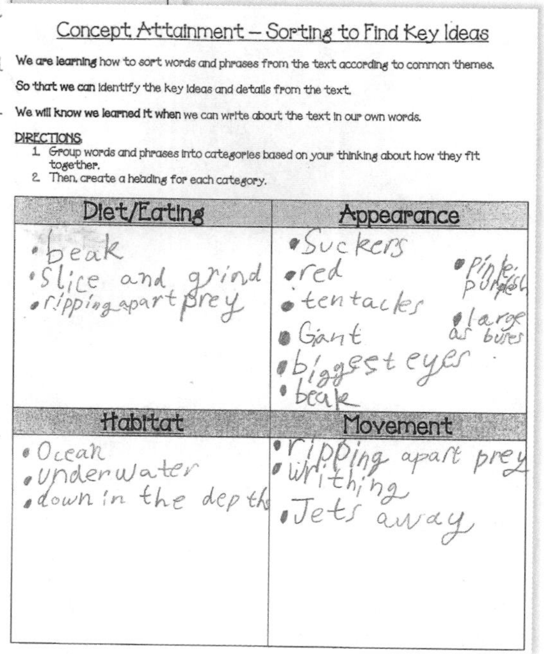

Concept Attainment – Sorting to Find Key Ideas

We are learning how to sort words and phrases from the text according to common themes.

So that we can identify the key ideas and details from the text.

We will know we learned it when we can write about the text in our own words.

DIRECTIONS:
1. Group words and phrases into categories based on your thinking about how they fit together.
2. Then, create a heading for each category.

Diet/Eating	Appearance	
• beak	• Suckers	• Pink purpsl
• Slice and grind	• red	
• ripping apart prey	• tentacles	• large as bus
	• Giant	
	• biggest eyes	
	• beak	

Habitat	Movement
• Ocean	• ripping apart prey
• underwater	• writhing
• down in the depth	• Jets away

Figure 4.15
As an added scaffold, provide students with category headings before they begin sorting.

- After their initial sorting is complete, students will read or listen to *Giant Squid*. During this second reading, students will be carefully reading or listening for additional words or phrases they can add to their existing groups. This reading might also prompt students to make some changes to their groupings or to the headings they have given to each group of words and phrases. Allow time during and after reading for students to make any necessary alterations to their work.

- Exit Slip–Students will choose one of their categories and explain it in their own words by writing a short informative piece or paragraph that draws on evidence from the text to convey the main idea and key details showcased in their chosen sorted category. (See Figure 4.16.)

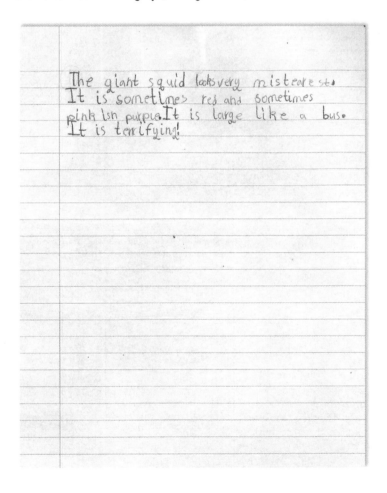

The giant squid looks very misteare st.
It is sometimes red and sometimes
pink ish purpla. It is large like a bus.
It is terrifying!

Figure 4.16
This student's paragraph about the giant squid's appearance uses words and phrases from the sorting activity.

Third Experience

CCSS: CCSS.ELA-Literacy.RI.2.7

- Begin this third session by asking students to recall and share their main ideas and details from the previous session. Connect this prior learning to the learning that will take place during the third reading of *Giant Squid* by teaching students that sometimes the illustrations connect with the words in ways that help readers better understand a text. Tell students that taking a closer look at the illustrations in *Giant Squid* will help them expand their understanding of the main ideas and details from the second reading.

- In this session, students will work together (in pairs, small groups, or as a whole class) to respond to text-dependent questions that require them to analyze the relationship between the text and the illustrations. Student discussion may also lead to a written response to one or a few of these questions, keeping in mind that shared writing as a class is always an option. For ease of reference, it is helpful to number the pages of the book using sticky notes so students can quickly access the pages.

- Possible Text-Dependent Question for Discussion

  ○ How does the title page (pages 6–7 spread) help you understand where the giant squid lives?

  ○ Why is the illustration on pages 12 and 13 important to the text?

  ○ How do the ink illustrations on pages 24–31 help you understand how the ink protects the giant squid from its predators?

  ○ Throughout the text the reader only sees parts of the giant squid on each page. At the end, the reader sees the whole giant squid, but it is gone quickly. Why do you think the author/illustrator made this choice? (See Figure 4.17.)

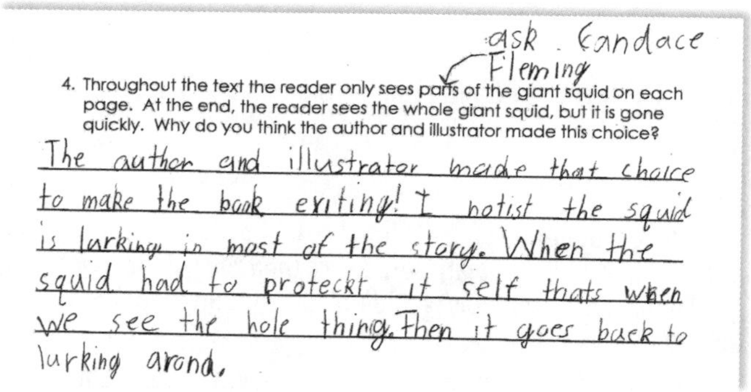

ask . Candace Fleming

4. Throughout the text the reader only sees parts of the giant squid on each page. At the end, the reader sees the whole giant squid, but it is gone quickly. Why do you think the author and illustrator made this choice?

The author and illustrator made that choice to make the book exiting! I notist the squid is lurking in most of the story. When the squid had to proteckt it self thats when we see the hole thing. Then it goes back to lurking arond.

Figure 4.17

A second-grade student's response to the text-dependent question that requires them to think about the choices that the author and illustrator made.

Fourth Experience
CCSS: CCSS.ELA-Literacy.RI.2.5, 2.7; CCSS.ELA-Literacy.W.2.1

- Introduce this session by calling attention to the end of the text that contains a diagram of the giant squid with labels and descriptions for each body part. Inform students that they are going to be zooming in on the diagram for this reading of the text. Discuss diagram as a text feature, and invite students to share their thinking about why a diagram is helpful in this (or any) text.
- Read aloud the diagram pages only, pausing for discussion as needed.
- Students will then reread or listen to the diagram pages in order to form and write an opinion about the body part they believe is most important to the giant squid's survival. Student opinions should draw on information from the diagram as well as from other pages of the text if necessary. (See Figure 4.18.)

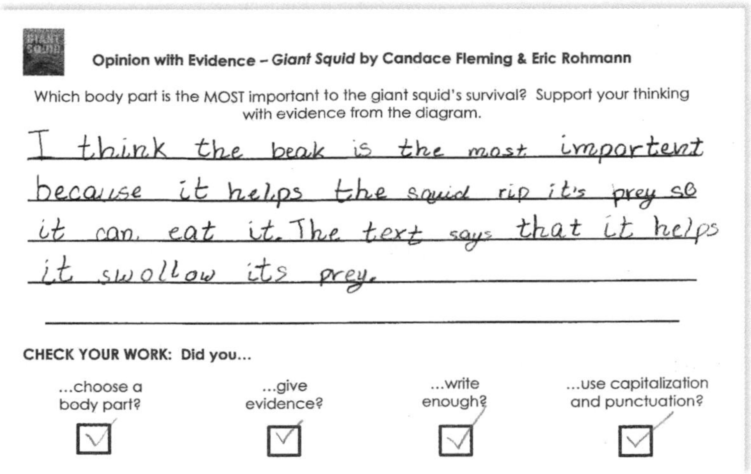

Opinion with Evidence – *Giant Squid* by Candace Fleming & Eric Rohmann

Which body part is the MOST important to the giant squid's survival? Support your thinking with evidence from the diagram.

I think the beak is the most important because it helps the squid rip it's prey so it can eat it. The text says that it helps it swollow its prey.

CHECK YOUR WORK: Did you...

...choose a body part?	...give evidence?	...write enough?	...use capitalization and punctuation?
☑	☑	☑	☑

Figure 4.18
This student supports his opinion with evidence from the diagram included in *Giant Squid*.

- A possible student response might be: I think the tentacles are most important because they help the giant squid suck their prey. If the giant squid did not have tentacles, it probably would not eat enough food. Then it would be hard for it to survive.
- To make thinking visible, each student can sign and place a small sticky note by the body part he or she deemed most important to the giant squid. Facilitate a class discussion based on student opinions, and allow time for students to share, compare, and debate their opinions with peers. (See Figure 4.19)

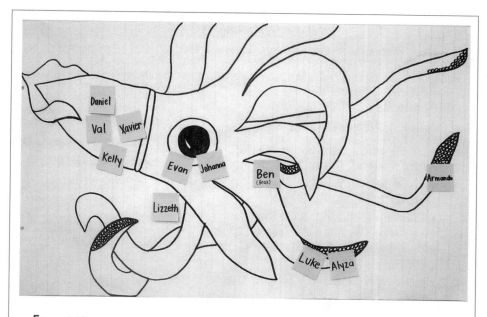

Figure 4.19
Students placed sticky notes on the giant squid to show their opinions and to spark discussion and debate within the close reading experience.

Fifth Experience and Culminating Task
CCSS: RI.2.1, RI.2.5

- Read aloud *Giant Squid* one last time or take students on a picture-walk through the book. This time, invite students to notice and share the kinds of information that the author includes. Keep a list of the kinds of facts (appearance, diet, habitat, etc.) and text features (diagram, author's note, title page, etc.) that make this book unique. Nudge students to think about how they could emulate these author and illustrator moves in their own writing.

- Possible Text-Dependent Questions for Discussion

  ○ Why do you think the author included these kinds of facts?

  ○ What text features are most important in this book?

  ○ How can we use this information to conduct our own research?

- Animal Research: Using close reading with *Giant Squid* provides the perfect launching point for students to conduct their own animal research. Students have had several experiences with this book and will now be able to use what they've learned to research and report on an animal of their choosing. Invite them to form their own questions and wonderings and as they get right to work creating a masterpiece like *Giant Squid*.

GRADE LEVEL: SECOND GRADE

TEXT: *YARD SALE* BY EVE BUNTING AND LAUREN CASTILLO (ILLUSTRATOR)

Background Information: *Yard Sale* is a can't-miss title for community building and empathy.

First Experience
CCSS: CCSS.ELA-Literacy.RL.2.1, 2.10

- Briefly introduce the story by reading the title and asking students to look closely at the front cover. What do they notice? What might this story be about?
- Read the book aloud, pausing minimally for discussion yet ensuring that students are following the story.
- Students will participate in a Share Your Thinking activity (see Chapter 2) that allows them to record their initial thoughts after reading this book. After students have had some time to write and draw their thinking, invite them to share their thinking with each other.
- Possible Text-Dependent Questions for Discussion

   ○ What is a yard sale?

   ○ Why is the family selling their stuff?

   ○ Where is the family moving to?

Second Experience
CCSS: CCSS.ELA-Literacy.RL.2.4

- This second session with *Yard Sale* will focus on the narration and dialogue that contribute to the overall mood of the story or the tone the author is trying to portray. Before beginning, ask students to recall their thinking from the first session, bringing back that initial layer of understanding before digging deeper.
- Introduce or review the idea of mood with students. Ask them to recall some books you've read together as a class that convey a happy or optimistic mood, and then some others that convey a sad or serious mood. Choose and display a few words, phrases, or sentences from the text that contribute to the overall mood (see the following table for a few examples). Invite students to share their thoughts on the mood that these chosen words convey. What do these words, phrases, and sentences have in common? What do they make you feel?

But it didn't feel like ours.
I wish I hadn't put the crayon marks on there.
"You can't take this," I say.
We have no place to keep it.

- As students read or listen to the text a second time, allow them to annotate and keep track of other words, sentences, and phrases that contribute to the mood of the story. This is a great opportunity to use Wikki Stix for annotation. After reading, compile a list on chart paper of all the words, phrases, or sentences that were annotated because they contribute to the mood. Ask students to revise or restate the overall mood of the story based on these annotations. Guide students to also notice how the mood shifts toward the end of the story. Annotate and discuss any narration or dialogue that helps convey this more optimistic mood and discuss how that shift in mood changes the story. (See Figure 4.20.)

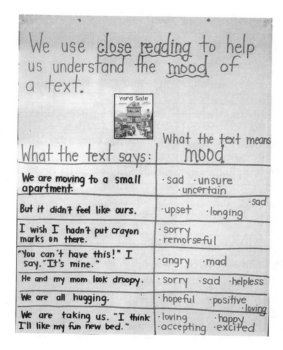

Figure 4.20
This chart shows students' understanding of the mood of the text based on the words and pictures it contains.

- Possible Text-Dependent Questions for Discussion

    ○ Why did the author choose to use these words?

    ○ How do these words help you understand what is happening?

    ○ How do these words make you feel when you read them?

    ○ How do these words help you know what the characters are feeling?

Third Experience

CCSS: CCSS.ELA-Literacy.RL.2.3

- During the third reading of *Yard Sale*, students will focus solely on the character Callie, keeping a close eye on her response to and feelings about the events taking place in her life. While reading the story, pause every few pages to record and discuss Callie's feelings. Annotate or record together any sentences or key words that provide evidence to support student thinking about Callie. After reading, facilitate a discussion about how Callie's feelings and emotions changed throughout the story and the events that prompted her to act or feel a certain way.

- Possible Text-Dependent Questions for Discussion

   ◦ What do you know about Callie because of what she does or says in the story?

   ◦ How did Callie's feelings change throughout the story?

- Written Response—After a thorough discussion about Callie, students will respond in their notebooks to one of the text-dependent questions listed here or to another question that requires them to synthesize their thinking about Callie. Another writing option is for students to journal about a time where they or someone they know experienced feelings similar to those of Callie.

Fourth Experience

CCSS: RL.2.2

- The final reading of *Yard Sale* combines the learning from the previous sessions so that students are able to determine the central message of the text.

- Revisit the learning materials (annotations, charts, responses) created throughout this reading experience. Inform students that they will be using their ideas about the mood of the story as well as their character clues from Callie in order to determine the central message of the story. Allow time for a group discussion about central message, reminding students that authors put a message into stories in different ways.

- Read the story a final time with the following question in students' minds: Based on Callie's thoughts and actions, what does the author want us to know after reading this book? After reading, respond to this question using a shared writing experience, inviting students to share text evidence that contributes to the central message of the story. Also take note of where the message comes in the story. In *Yard Sale,* the big message comes toward the end of the story, but Eve Bunting tucks in smaller (yet still powerful) messages throughout the story as well. Teach students that authors can sneak their messages into stories in many places, so readers must always be on the lookout!

- Take the learning a step further by asking students what this text means to them as second graders. How has this book changed something inside of you? What have you learned from Callie's experience?

I hope these ideas and suggestions for using close reading in the classroom have sparked an interest or an "I can totally do that!" mentality (because you totally can!). These experiences with close reading have worked for me, and I believe they make a difference for kids, but putting your own individual spin on them makes them all the more powerful for the readers you learn with each day. Take my ideas and make them work for you. To echo the wise words of Anne Marie Corgill in *Of Primary Importance*, "think of this book as a friend standing by to cheer you on in your classroom" (2008, 3). Let me be that friend you wish you had more time to collaborate with during planning time if you weren't so busy responding to parent emails, collecting student data, and (dare I say it?) going to the bathroom.

As you start to look at close reading through a new lens, don't forget about all the reasons you love teaching young children to read in the first place. Close reading fits right inside all those things you hold dear to your hearts. Your favorite characters, topics, and books will not disappear; they will become more alive as you guide your students to think about things in new ways, to grab on to big understandings and grow as readers. Your young readers will shine as they work with texts that stretch their thinking, empower them to take ownership of their learning, and inspire them to tackle new goals. Close reading is one of the best opportunities we have for our little readers to showcase just how big their thinking can be. Believe in your little readers as much as they believe in you.

5

Closing Thoughts

Remember then, with every try,
sometimes you fail . . . sometimes you fly.
—KATHERINE APPLEGATE, *SOMETIMES YOU FLY*

At the end of the day, we have to ask ourselves if the reading practices we value in our classrooms reflect the readers we want our students to become and the reading that takes place in the world. Do we provide our little readers with enough opportunities to notice, wonder, think, play, and talk while reading? Are we teaching them the skills that real readers use?

We strive each day to make our classrooms places of wonder, places of exploration, places of discovery. The reading experiences we make possible for our students should be no different. When we teach students how to closely examine a text, we are teaching them that there is always more to notice. We are teaching them to harness their senses of wonder and to let that wonderment lead the way to learning. We are equipping our young readers with new tools to keep in their reading toolboxes, so that they can begin to notice, wonder, and explore in all the books they read. Close reading should provide a platform through which students' natural curiosity can be set free. Look for little ways to honor and invite wonder during reading experiences. After all, isn't wonder the foundation of all learning?

This book outlines a framework for close reading that builds on what students can do and what you are already doing as teachers. Armed with an initial understanding of what happens when they read like detectives, students begin to think about reading in a different way and dig a little deeper right from the start. Teaching students how to be expert noticers sets the stage for rich discussions and honors readers' different perspectives, ideas, and ways of thinking.

As young readers work through multiple experiences with a text, their understanding deepens, their curiosity takes over, and their learning becomes more meaningful, leading them to become deeper thinkers in areas and aspects of their lives that extend beyond reading in the classroom. Text-dependent questions and text-based learning that elicit understanding and increasingly challenge readers to draw on their thinking about the text and about the world beyond the text are an invaluable part of the close reading process. Discussions and thinking that arise from these reading experiences fuel the rigor and complexity of the reading experience. It is up to you to decide what close reading looks like in your classroom and what it means for your little readers. The ideas in this book are meant to support and celebrate the close reading work you do with children throughout the year.

■ Close Reading Is a Balancing Act

As you begin or continue a close reading journey in your classroom, remember that balance is key. Just as we balance the many hats we wear at school (and I mean many hats), so too must we balance many aspects of teaching reading. There is a time and a place for close reading. We use close reading when a text is worthy of more than just a surface-level understanding. We use close reading when the content challenges students to elevate the level of their thinking. We use close reading when we seize an opportunity to invite students to get to know an author or illustrator deeply.

There is also a time and place for just good old-fashioned reading. We must never let go of reading books just for the fun of it. The simple joy of reading and of being read to are what keep us coming back for more books—new titles as well as old favorites. Close reading strategies do not compromise all the other pieces of reading instruction that bring us so much joy. Rather, they weave a variety of reading skills and strategies into a cohesive framework with children in mind and a text at the core. It is a delicate balancing act, but it means nothing if we lose the love, joy, and passion for reading along the way. And who knows, you just might find that close reading will add a new kind of joy to your classroom.

■ Rethinking Time: Be Stingy and Critical

I know there's no time. I live in the Land of Zero Time right alongside you, and I have to consciously stop myself from uttering "There's just no time!" at least fifty times a day. My intention with this book is to frame (or reframe) close reading for you as a meaningful, manageable practice worthy of the precious time we have with our students. We can choose spend that time in inauthentic, disconnected instruction, or we can choose to spend that time engaged in student-driven instruction, including real reading, organic thinking, and deep conversation. I think you will agree that the latter is much more productive and a lot more fun.

Earlier in this book I share my thoughts on the misconstruction of close reading by people who have never lived in our primary world (or, quite frankly, in any classroom). What has often been made out to be a long and laborious process for both teachers and students is not actually how it has to be. A quick, text-based discussion question during a morning meeting—that's close reading. A dive back into a book to find and mark three words that start with *c*—that's close reading. A turn-and-talk opportunity to share feelings after reading a powerful text—that's close reading. Returning to a favorite read-aloud book to do more noticing—that's close reading. Instead of one more thing to do, think of it as a way to combine and refine the reading your students are already doing.

Knowing that close reading is an essential skill for real readers, we must be thoughtful about what it looks like in the primary grades. Where are our students and what kind of complexity and rigor make sense for them as readers? In their book *Purposeful Play*, Kristine Mraz, Alison Porcelli, and Cheryl Tyler define rigor as "big thinking in child-friendly ways" (2016, 4). I love this for many reasons, but mostly because it puts kids first. Teaching students to think big in ways that are meaningful for them is a central tenet of close reading.

We must also take up a critical stance on the kinds of instruction being mandated or prohibited and advocate for students who are not yet able to advocate for themselves. Decide what is unnecessarily taking up your instructional or planning time, and eliminate it. Time with—and preparing for—our little readers who are their most curious and most absorbent selves cannot be wasted.

■ Rise Up to Meet Challenges

It is no secret that the children with whom we learn each day face increasing challenges. Sometimes these challenges hinder students' progress toward goals or work against students' belief in themselves as thinkers and learners. Our task as teachers is to combat these challenges by providing connective, meaningful experiences that showcase all that our students are capable of. If we do not give our little readers and writers opportunities to learn that their thoughts and words—their big thinking—matter, it is quite possible they will continue in their schooling without realizing that their voices are powerful.

When we craft opportunities for close reading with students' input in mind, we show students that we value their thinking as important and celebrate the deep comprehension—of the text and beyond—that takes place for them as readers. Sometimes all our little readers need is a little love, a good book, and an I-believe-in-you nudge. As you return to your classroom, let this book serve as your I-believe-in-you nudge toward new close reading experiences with your young readers.

Teachers also face many challenges. Some of us work in buildings with few resources to support our teaching. Some of us have been mandated to teach a curriculum that is so scripted we've lost all our professional autonomy, leaving us feeling powerless and unsure about the disciplines in which we once considered ourselves experts. Some of us work tirelessly under leaders whose educational values differ from our own. Close reading will not solve all our problems, but we can use it as a means to work around some of these challenges. It is my hope that close reading focused on student needs and thinking will help us to transcend these challenges, and that in teaching our students to let their voices be heard, we remember to also use our own.

■ Spread the Joy

Reading is a gift we give our students. It is a gift wrapped in compelling characters, wondrous words, and incredible information. Close reading is a way to bring those characters, words, and pieces of information to life in new, joyful ways for our students. It is a window to themselves and the world around them. When we invite children to return to a text for more noticing or wondering, we are teaching our little readers that there is always time to hear what they have to say. When we take a closer look to describe a character from a story, we are teaching them the importance of individuality and of learning about others. When we annotate a text to signal words containing a pattern we've learned, we are teaching them that their knowledge is not isolated, but far-reaching. When we read in different ways and for different purposes, we are teaching them to find more to love in the texts they read.

Reading, thinking, and learning are joyful experiences. Let this book serve as your invitation to seize that joy through close reading. You are invited to see the practice of close reading in a different light, to try something new, or to revisit a beloved text in new ways. Recognize that success with close reading might come little by little, but with each tweak of our instruction or each nudge toward deeper thinking comes great rewards for readers. The more we practice, the better we get. The same is true for our young readers. Students may be reluctant to share and discuss their big thinking at first, but when we celebrate that thinking across several reading experiences within a safe community of thinkers, it will make itself more and more visible. Notice what your readers can do, even if they can't yet read the words on their own.

Reading closely is a skill that students will ultimately keep with them and use for the rest of their lives, and the inspiration to read with a close eye or listen with a close ear begins in the first years of school. Encouraging close, passionate, engaged, real readers starts when they are little. It is our job as primary-grade teachers to provide guidance, support, and reading experiences that will elevate our students' thinking. As we have learned from Vygotsky, "What the child can do in cooperation today, he can do alone tomorrow" (1989, 189). Close reading in the primary grades is cooperative; we work together with our students to help them discover all a text has to offer and everything that reading can be. Close reading encourages young readers to be deep thinkers both inside and outside of the classroom. Introducing students to close reading at a young age means they will grow up with skills that will enable them to look not only at books but also at life, people, and events with greater insight and wisdom.

When it comes time for us to send our students out the door at the end of the year, we must know that we have done all we can do set them up for joy and success as readers. As much as we want to keep them close—to keep them little—there comes a time when we have to let them fly. And if we've done our jobs, fly they will. Just like Rosie Revere in her cheese-copter, whirling round and round in *Rosie Revere, Engineer* by Andrea Beaty. Just like Penguin at the end of *Flight School*, soaring on the wind. Just like Jabari, cutting through the air after his jump off of the high diving board in *Jabari Jumps*. Your little readers will soar to become big readers. They have always had their wings, but you, dear teacher, have shown them how to fly.

appendix a

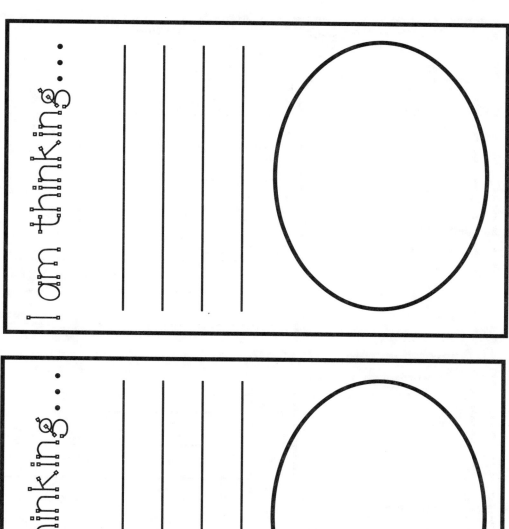

appendix b

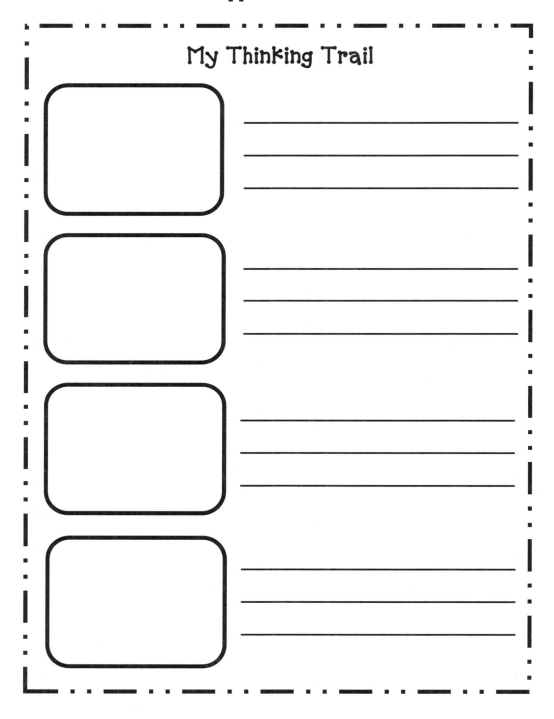

My Thinking Trail

appendix c

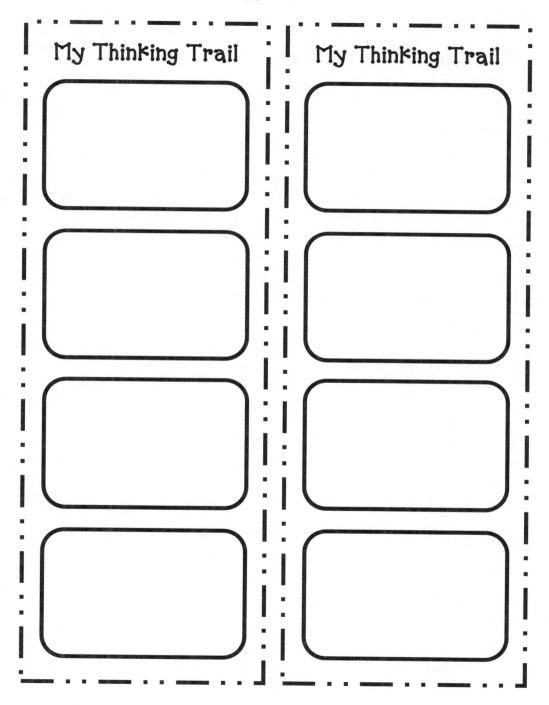

appendix d

I Am a Word Detective!

New Word	What I THINK It Means	What It REALLY Means	How I Know

appendix e

New Word:

_____

- -

_____

From this text . . .

> Place photo
> of front
> cover of the
> text here.

What does it mean?

_____

- -

_____

- -

_____

An illustration of the new word . . .

A. Stewart 2016

appendix f

I am a Pizza

I am a pizza   C
With extra cheese   G
From tomatoes   G
Sauce is squeezed   C
Garlic and mushrooms   F
Oregano   G
I am a pizza . . . ready to go!   Am-F-C, G7-C

I am a pizza
Pepperoni
No anchovies
Or phony balogna
Onions and sausage
Order by phone
I am a pizza . . . take me home!

I am a pizza
With fresh baked crust.
I am a pizza . . . ready to bust!

I am a pizza
Peppers on top
Out of the oven
Into the box
Into the car and
Upside-down
I am a pizza . . . dropped on the ground

I was a pizza   C
I was the best   Dm
I was a pizza . . . now I'm a mess!   Am-F-C, G7-C

references

Beers, Kylene, and Robert E. Probst. 2013. *Notice and Note: Strategies for Close Reading*. Portsmouth, NH: Heinemann.

———. 2015. *Reading Nonfiction: Notice & Note Stances, Signposts, and Strategies*. Portsmouth, NH: Heinemann.

Boyles, Nancy. 2014. "Close Reading Without Tears." *Educational Leadership* 72 (1): 32–37.

Britton, James. 1970. *Language and Learning*. Coral Gables, FL: University of Miami Press.

Chall, Jeanne S. 1983. *Stage of Reading Development*. New York: McGraw-Hill.

Collins, Kathy, and Matt Glover. 2015. *I Am Reading*: *Nurturing Young Children's Meaning Making and Joyful Engagement with Any Book*. Portsmouth, NH: Heinemann.

Corgill, Ann M. 2008 *Of Primary Importance: What's Essential in Teaching Young Writers*. Portland, ME: Stenhouse.

Cunningham, Patricia. 2009. *What Really Matters in Vocabulary: Research-Based Practices Across the Curriculum*. New York: Pearson.

Daniels, Harvey. 2017. *The Curious Classroom: 10 Structures for Teaching with Student-Directed Inquiry*. Portsmouth, NH: Heinemann.

Fisher, Doug, and Nancy Frey. 2012. "Close Reading in Elementary Schools." *The Reading Teacher* 66 (3): 179–88.

———. 2014a. "Close Reading Up Close." Corwin. https://us.corwin.com/en-us/nam/webinar/close-reading-up-close.

———. 2014b. *Text-Dependent Questions: Pathways to Close and Critical Reading.* Thousand Oaks, CA: Corwin.

Fisher, Doug, Nancy Frey, and Diane Lapp. 2011. *Teaching Students to Read Like Detectives: Comprehending, Analyzing, and Discussing Text.* Bloomington, IN: Solution Tree Press.

———. 2012. *Text Complexity: Raising Rigor in Reading.* Newark, DE: International Reading Association.

Johnston, Peter. 2004. *Choice Words: How Our Language Affects Children's Learning.* Portland ME: Stenhouse.

Kagan, Spencer, and Miguel Kagan. 2015. *Kagan Cooperative Learning Strategies.* San Clemente, CA: Kagan Learning.

Layne, Steven. 2009. *Igniting a Passion for Reading: Successful Strategies for Building Lifetime Readers.* Portland, ME: Stenhouse.

Lehman, Christopher, and Kate Roberts. 2014. *Falling in Love with Close Reading: Lessons for Analyzing Texts—and Life.* Portsmouth, NH: Heinemann.

Macon, James M., Diane Bewell, and MaryEllen Vogt. 1991. *Responses to Literature: Grades K–8.* Newark, DE: International Reading Association.

Miller, Debbie. 2002. *Happy Reading! Creating a Predictable Structure for Joyful Teaching and Learning.* Video. Portland, ME: Stenhouse.

———. 2012. *Reading with Meaning: Teaching Comprehension in the Primary Grades.* 3rd ed. Portland, ME: Stenhouse.

Moses, Lindsey, and Meridith Ogden. 2017. *What Are the Rest of My Kids Doing? Fostering Independence in the K–2 Reading Workshop.* Portsmouth, NH: Heinemann.

Mraz, Kristine, Allison Porcelli, and Cheryl Tyler. 2016. *Purposeful Play: A Teacher's Guide to Igniting Deep and Joyful Learning Across the Day.* Portsmouth, NH: Heinemann.

National Governors Association Center for Best Practices and Council of Chief State School Officers. 2010. *Common Core State Standards for English Language Arts and Literacy in History/Social Studies, Science, and Technical Subjects.* Washington, DC: Authors.

Pearson, P. D., and M. C. Gallagher. 1983. "The Instruction of Reading Comprehension." *Contemporary Educational Psychology* 8: 317–44.

Rosenblatt, Louise. 1978. *The Reader, the Text, the Poem: The Transactional Theory of Literary Work*. Carbondale, IL: Southern Illinois University.

Serravallo, Jennifer. 2015. *The Reading Strategies Book: Your Everything Guide to Developing Skilled Readers*. Portsmouth, NH: Heinemann.

Vygotsky, Lev. 1989. *Thought and Language*. Cambridge, MA: MIT Press.

Walther, Maria. 2015. *Transforming Literacy Teaching in the Era of Higher Standards: Model Lessons and Practical Strategies That Show You How to Integrate the Standards to Plan and Teach with Confidence*. New York: Scholastic.

■ Children's Literature Cited

Aillaud, Cindy Lou. 2005. *Recess at 20 Below*. Portland, OR: Alaska Northwest Books.

Applegate, Katherine. 2014. *Ivan: The Remarkable True Story of the Shopping Mall Gorilla*. Illus. G. Brian Karas. Boston: Clarion Books.

Arnold, Tedd. 2016. *Fly Guy Presents: Weather*. New York: Scholastic.

Arnosky, Jim. 2008. *Wild Tracks! A Guide to Nature's Footprints*. New York: Sterling Children's Books.

Baker, Jeannie. 2010. *Mirror*. Somerville, MA: Candlewick.

Barnett, Mac, and Jon Klassen. 2014. *Sam and Dave Dig a Hole*. Somerville, MA: Candlewick.

————. 2017. *Triangle*. Somerville, MA: Candlewick.

Barton, Bethany. 2017. *Give Bees a Chance*. New York: Viking Books for Young Readers.

Beaty, Andrea. 2013. *Rosie Revere, Engineer*. Illus. David Roberts. New York: Harry N. Abrams.

Becker, Aaron. 2013. *Journey*. Somerville, MA: Candlewick.

Biedrzycki, David. 2008. *Ace Lacewing: Bug Detective*. Watertown, MA: Charlesbridge.

Birney, Betty G. 2005. *The World According to Humphrey*. New York: Puffin Books.

Bishop, Nic. 2007. *Spiders*. New York: Scholastic.

Brown, Peter. 2013. *Mr. Tiger Goes Wild.* Boston: Little, Brown.

Bunting, Eve. 2015. *Yard Sale*. Illus. Lauren Castillo. Somerville, MA: Candlewick.

Clement, Rod. 1997. *Grandpa's Teeth.* New York: HarperCollins.

Cole, Henry. 2012. *Unspoken*. New York: Scholastic.

———. 2016. *Spot, the Cat*. New York: Little Simon.

Cornwall, Gaia. 2017. *Jabari Jumps.* Somerville, MA: Candlewick.

Cowcher, Helen. 2011. *Desert Elephants*. New York: Farrar, Straus and Giroux.

Daywalt, Drew. 2013. *The Day the Crayons Quit.* Illus. Oliver Jeffers. New York: Philomel Books.

DeDonato, Rick. 2016. *Pipsie, Nature Detective: The Lunchnapper*. Illus. Tracy Bishop. New York: Two Lions.

Diamond, Charlotte. "I Am a Pizza." Recorded September 1985. Track 11 on *10 Carrot Diamond*. Hug Bug Records. Compact disc.

Dotlich, Rebecca Kai. 2015. *One Day, The End: Short, Very Short, Shorter-Than-Ever Stories*. Illus. Fred Koehler. Honesdale, PA: Boyds Mills Press.

Engle, Margarita. 2017. *Bravo! Poems About Amazing Hispanics*. Illus. Rafael López. New York: Henry Holt.

Falatko, Julie. 2016. *Snappsy the Alligator: Who Did Not Ask to Be in This Book.* Illus. Tim Miller. New York: Viking Books for Young Readers.

Fan, Terry, and Eric Fan. 2016. *The Night Gardener*. New York: Simon & Schuster Books for Young Readers.

Fleming, Candace. 2016. *Giant Squid*. Illus. Eric Rohmann. New York: Roaring Brook Press.

Foreman, Michael. 2011. *Fortunately, Unfortunately.* London: Andersen Press Picture Books.

Funk, Josh. 2015. *Lady Pancake and Sir French Toast: The Case of the Stinky Stench.* Illus. Brendan Kearney. New York: Sterling Children's Books.

Goldsaito, Katrina. 2016. *The Sound of Silence*. Illus. Julia Kuo. New York: Little, Brown Books for Young Readers.

Heling, Kathryn, and Deborah Hembrook. 2012. *Clothesline Clues to Jobs People Do*. Illus. Andy Robert Davies. Watertown, MA: Charlesbridge.

Jeffers, Oliver. 2017. *Here We Are: Notes for Living on Planet Earth*. New York: Philomel Books.

Jenkins, Steve, and Robin Page. 2015. *How to Swallow a Pig: Step-by-Step Advice from the Animal Kingdom*. New York: HMH Books for Young Readers.

John, Jory. 2017. *The Bad Seed*. Illus. Pete Oswald. New York: HarperCollins.

Judge, Lita. 2014. *Flight School*. New York: Atheneum Books for Young Readers.

Kang, Anna. 2014. *You Are (Not) Small*. Illus. Christopher Weyant. New York: Two Lions.

Keating, Jess. 2016. *Pink Is for Blobfish: Discovering the World's Perfectly Pink Animals*. Illus. David DeGrand. The World of Weird Animals series. New York: Knopf Books for Young Readers.

Keats, Ezra Jack. 1962. *The Snowy Day*. New York: Viking Press.

Lawson, JonArno. 2015. *Sidewalk Flowers*. Illus. Sydney Smith. Toronto: Groundwood Books.

Lee, Suzy. 2008. *Wave*. San Francisco: Chronicle Books.

Levinson, Cynthia. 2017. *The Youngest Marcher: The Story of Audrey Faye Hendricks, a Young Civil Rights Activist*. Illus. Vanessa Brantley Newton. New York: Atheneum Books for Young Readers.

Lloyd, Jennifer. 2013. *Murilla Gorilla, Jungle Detective*. Illus. Jacqui Lee. Vancouver, BC: Simply Read Books.

Matsuoka, Mai. 2008. *Footprints in the Snow*. New York: Henry Holt.

Olien, Jessica. 2015. *Shark Detective!* New York: Balzer and Bray.

Paul, Miranda. 2015. *One Plastic Bag: Isatou Ceesay and the Recycling Women of the Gambia*. Illus. Elizabeth Zunon. Minneapolis, MN: Millbrook Press.

Paul, Miranda. 2015. *Whose Hands Are These? A Community Helper Guessing Book*. Illus. Luciana Navarro Powell. Minneapolis, MN: Millbrook Press.

Pett, Mark. 2014. *The Girl and the Bicycle*. New York: Simon and Schuster Books for Young Readers.

Pinkney, Jerry. 2009. *The Lion and the Mouse*. New York: Little, Brown.

Ramsey, Alexander, and Gwen Strauss. 2010. *Ruth and the Green Book*. Illus. Floyd Cooper. Minneapolis, MN: Carolrhoda Books.

Reynolds, Peter H. 2003. *The Dot*. New York: Scholastic.

Roberts, Justin. 2014. *The Smallest Girl in the Smallest Grade*. Illus. Christian Robinson. New York: G. P. Putnam's Sons Books for Young Readers.

Rocco, John. 2011. *Blackout*. White Plains, NY: Disney-Hyperion.

———. 2014. *Blizzard*. White Plains, NY: Disney-Hyperion.

Selsam, Millicent E. 1991. *Big Tracks, Little Tracks: Following Animal Prints*. Illus. Marlene Hill Donnelly. New York: HarperCollins.

Selznick, Brian, and David Serlin. 2018. *Baby Monkey, Private Eye*. New York: Scholastic.

Serafini, Frank. 2014. *Looking Closely Through the Forest*. Toronto: Kids Can Press.

Shannon, David. 1998. *No, David!* New York: Blue Sky Press.

Sharmat, Marjorie Weinman. 1982. *Nate the Great*. Illus. Marc Simont. New York: Yearling.

———. 1982. *Nate the Great and the Snowy Trail*. Illus. Marc Simont. New York: Yearling.

Shea, Bob. 2015. *Ballet Cat: The Totally Secret Secret*. White Plains, NY: Disney-Hyperion.

Sierra, Judy. 2008. *Born to Read*. Illus. Marc Brown. New York: Alfred A. Knopf.

Spires, Ashley. 2014. *The Most Magnificent Thing*. Tonawanda, NY: Kids Can Press.

Steptoe, John. 2008. *Mufaro's Beautiful Daughters*. New York: Puffin Books.

Tallec, Olivier. 2015. *Who Done It?* San Francisco: Chronicle Books.

———. 2016. *Who What Where?* San Francisco: Chronicle Books.

Teague, Mark. 2004. *Detective LaRue: Letters from the Investigation*. New York: Scholastic.

Thomson, Bill. 2010. *Chalk*. New York: Two Lions.

Willems, Mo. 2003. *Don't Let the Pigeon Drive the Bus!* Burbank, CA: Disney.

——. 2013. *That Is NOT a Good Idea!* Elephant and Piggie series. New York: Balzer and Bray.

——. 2014. *Waiting Is Not Easy*. White Plains, NY: Disney-Hyperion.

——.Woodson, Jacqueline. 2012. *Each Kindness*. New York: Nancy Paulsen Books.

Yee, Wong Herbert. 2003. *Tracks in the Snow*. New York: Square Fish.